667.3　　Scheiner, Paul
Sch

　　　　$5 Cup of Coffee is Ruining M
　　　　retirement

Property of
Congregation Beth Shalom
Library
772 West 5th Ave.
Naperville, IL 60543-2948

DEMCO

The $5 Cup of Coffee is Ruining My Retirement

Saving for Retirement

Paul Scheiner, BSE, MSE

Copyright © 2008 by Paul Scheiner, BSE, MSE.

ISBN: Hardcover   978-1-4363-4886-7
              Softcover   978-1-4363-4885-0

All rights reserved. No part of this book may be reproduced or transmitted in any form or by any means, electronic or mechanical, including photocopying, recording, or by any information storage and retrieval system, without permission in writing from the copyright owner.

This book was printed in the United States of America.

To order additional copies of this book, contact:
Xlibris Corporation
1-888-795-4274
www.Xlibris.com
Orders@Xlibris.com
50335

Contents

Acknowledgement 5
Preface 7
Introduction 9
Chapter 1—The New Retirement 13
    1.1   The Older Generation 14
    1.2   The Baby Boomers 16
    1.3   The Now Generation 21
    1.4   Why Can't They All be Successful? 25
Chapter 2—What Changed? 27
    2.1   Pensions 28
    2.2   Social Security 30
    2.3   Savings 32
    2.4   Early Retirement by Choice? 34
    2.5   What are the Real Choices? 34
Chapter 3—The Fruit of Your Labor—Avoid Working in Retirement 36
    3.1   Why Do We Work? 38
    3.2   Selecting Leisure Activities 40
    3.3   The Magic Lists 41
    3.4   The Healthy Lifestyle 44
    3.5   Travel 46
    3.6   Sense of Accomplishment 47
    3.7   Should you work part-time? 48
Chapter 4—Can You Afford to Retire? 50
    4.1   Life Expectancy 51
    4.2   How to Estimate the Required Size of Your Nest Egg? 53
    4.3   Retirement Planner 57
    4.4   Suppose You Can't Afford to Retire 58
Chapter 5—Turning it All Around 61
    5.1   Getting into Debt 63
    5.2   Getting Out of Debt 64
    5.3   Avoiding Temptation 66
    5.4   Managing Spending—Cutting Waste 69
    5.5   Paying off Your debts 71
Chapter 6—Stop Wasting Away Your Future 74
    6.1   Giving Them the Best 75
    6.2   Transportation 77
    6.3   Entertainment 79
    6.4   Food and Drugs 84
    6.5   Let's Get Physical 87
    6.6   Miscellaneous Consumer Expenses 89
    6.7   Your Personal Savings Scorecard 92

Chapter 7—Saving for Your Future 94
    7.1   The Miracle of Compounding 95
    7.2   The Value of Starting Early 97
    7.3   The Ravages of Inflation 98
    7.4   Pay Yourself First 99
    7.5   Retire a Millionaire.. 100

Chapter 8—Managing Your Money... 102
    8.1   Pre-Tax Accounts 103
    8.2   Workplace 401(k) Plans.. 104
    8.3   Personal Tax Deferred Accounts 109
    8.4   Personal Investment Accounts 114
    8.5   Certificates of Deposit and Government Bonds........... 115
    8.6   Tying it All Together.. 118

Chapter 9—Investing Your Money 119
    9.1   Managing Your Own Money... 119
    9.2   Professional Investment Advice 121
    9.3   Risk.. 123
    9.4   Overcoming Fear.. 127
    9.5   Saving, Speculating, and Investing................................ 128
    9.6   The Stock Market 129
    9.7   What is a Share of Stock?... 131
    9.8   What is a Mutual Fund? 131

Chapter 10—Growing Your Nest Egg—Investing 101 134
    10.1   Critical Factors—The Dirty Four and Five Letter Words. 135
    10.2   Guidelines for Successful Investing 136
    10.3   Asset Allocation and Diversification............................ 138
    10.4   Personalizing Your Plan... 141
    10.5   Investing in Stocks 143
    10.6   Investing in Bonds.. 150
    10.7   Cash Investments.. 152
    10.8   Index Funds.. 153
    10.9   Balancing Your Funds... 154

Chapter 11—Early Retirement... 158
    11.1   The Window of Opportunity...................................... 159
    11.2   Advantages of Retiring Early 161
    11.3   Disadvantages of Retiring Early.................................. 162
    11.4   Health Insurance... 165

Chapter 12—Outliving Your Money 169
    12.1   Spending Early vs. Spending Later.............................. 170
    12.2   Controlling Discretionary Spending 171
    12.3   Living the Simple Life 176
    12.4   Spending Down Your Nest Egg 177

Chapter 13—Myths and Realities... 180

Acknowledgement

My thanks and appreciation goes out to my daughter, April Scheiner, for serving as a sounding board for many of the concepts presented. Her efforts made it possible for this book to be written. Her fine editing work is also greatly appreciated.

Preface

I stopped at a bagel take-out store to pick up a dozen bagels for a family brunch. The store had an upscale coffee bar near the entrance. I was amazed to see the long line of people waiting to purchase their $5 cups of coffee and a pricey muffin. Watching them, it dawned on me that habits like these are making it so difficult for people to retire at 65 years of age. That experience resulted in the origin of "The $5 Cup of Coffee is Ruining My Retirement".

Coming from a relatively poor family, I never had much money in my wallet. I learned to be frugal and typically spent the money that I did have on necessities. The idea of investing money was such a foreign concept that I didn't even know what it meant until I was 35 years old. My frugal lifestyle enabled me to save money and start investing in my thirties. I started out investing conservatively. When I learned more about the financial world, I began investing more aggressively. I made a number of mistakes along the way, but managed to learn from each and make wiser decisions in the future. Now that I'm approaching retirement, I find myself financially as well as socially well prepared. I feel compelled to pass along my lessons learned to benefit others who will likewise be entering the confusing world of spending, saving, and investing.

"The $5 Cup of Coffee is Ruining My Retirement" is a primer on the financial and social aspects of preparing for, and living in, retirement. This book provides the insights that you will need to reduce your spending, pay down your debts, and build your wealth so that retirement will be the best time of your life. Developing and acting on your plans for retirement is the key. There is plenty of hope, no matter what your present financial situation. Don't get discouraged. **But you must start now!**

The subject matter covered in this book will fill in many of the gaps in your financial understanding. It will teach you how to develop your own personalized financial plan. You will learn the necessity of lifestyle changes to eliminate waste and pay off debt in order to start building your nest egg. There are chapters aimed at providing novice investors with a basic understanding of investments and how to safely increase the value of their assets. Furthermore, "The $5 Cup of Coffee is Ruining My Retirement" explores a number of social issues associated with leaving the job force, selecting leisure activities, and controlling spending in the retirement years. This is a book that you will want to keep on your shelf for reference over the years.

Introduction

Not too many years ago retirement was a short bridge between life and death. Retirement was considered a heaven-sent gift for an employee who, after 40 years of work, had become too tired, burned out, or sickly to work any longer. Today things are very different. The wonders of modern medicine combined with preventive methods to avoid illness have extended the lives of most of the population and, in turn, has added many years to retirement.

People in reasonably good health at the age of 60 can now expect to live close to thirty more years. These can be the happiest years of their lives, since the pressures of earning a living, building a career, and raising a family are behind them. Workers can use their "golden years" to do many of the things they had always hoped to do, but never had the opportunity to do because of their 40 plus hour work weeks. Unfortunately, the cost of these additional retirement years can present a problem if there is insufficient financial preparation. Therefore, a retirement plan needs to be set in motion at an early stage of life to assure that retirement is all that it can be.

Employees always expected the two old standbys of retirement income: Social Security and corporate pensions to provide the financial independence necessary to support them through their retirement years. Presently a majority of retirees depend on Social Security for at least half, if not all, of their retirement income. Meanwhile, the Social Security Program is being challenged by the longer life expectancy of retirees, resulting in more retirees being supported by a diminishing work force. Although Social Security will continue to cover retirees, the program will probably require future cutbacks and subsequently less generous payouts in the future.

At the same time, corporate pensions are quickly becoming a relic of the past. Not only are very few companies still offering pensions to new employees but many companies are also scaling back their commitments to older workers by freezing their pension plans. This makes the employee unable to continue to accumulate pension benefits. Therefore, future retirees will obtain either scaled back pensions or no pensions at all, leaving them to rely primarily on Social Security. Make no mistake about it; Social Security will not be enough.

Earning a living, raising a family, and keeping yourself and your loved ones happy is more than a full-time endeavor for most people. Preparing for retirement when it's still twenty or thirty years away just isn't a very high priority to the average worker. Hence, it is no wonder that so many workers have not bothered to implement plans to grow their nest eggs in order to live comfortably in their later years. Workers will need to work longer than planned and therefore will miss out on many of the joys of the golden years.

Have you saved very little so far and have nothing to show for it but debts and credit card bills? Do you feel like you can't save a dime because of the demands of a growing family? From where will the rest of the money come? Will it come from savings? Unfortunately 50% of American workers have saved less than $50,000 for retirement, including a good number of those already over 55 years of age. Many of the soon-to-be retirees are in debt due to reliance on credit cards, car loans and unexpected expenses that remain unpaid. The savings will not be there for these people when they reach retirement age. One in four of our wealthiest generation, the baby boomers, will not have sufficient funds to retire as planned.

What will retirees do to compensate for the lack of funds? Future generations will need to change their habits and begin the planning and saving stage early in their lifetimes. For many who are approaching the retirement years, it may be too late. They are now becoming aware of the need to keep working in order to provide the income they will need for their later years. Younger workers still have the opportunity to make changes in their lifestyles to prepare themselves adequately for retirement. All that is really needed are attitude and lifestyle adjustments. If you are in your forties or even early fifties there is still adequate time to change so that you will be able to stop working and retire debt-free at the age of 65. The time to act is now.

This book is directed at those who have the willingness to change their patterns of waste and grow their nest eggs for the times ahead. The following chapters will provide guidance to readers through a process that should indeed make retirement the "time of their lives"

Chapter 1

The New Retirement

Today's retirement challenges are distinctly different from those that our fathers and grandfathers faced. Both would typically work to age 65 and then live off their pensions and Social Security for a few years before disease, poor health, and/or old age caused their passing. Due to their short life expectancy, the financial needs of this group of retirees were not excessive. They were in poorer health, had less energy and less desire for travel than the modern retiree and were often content to sit home, putter around the house, and watch television.

In the past, it was unusual for the main breadwinner to live much beyond 70 years of age. Today, with increased longevity, a 60-year-old couple can expect an additional 30-year lifespan for at least one of them. They will need to save a large sum of money or will face an unfulfilling retirement and possibly even be forced to live with relatives. The Social Security system was designed to pay for a retiree's necessities such as food and shelter. If the worker had a pension from his/her employer, as many did, the retirement years could be reasonably comfortable. Inflation would not have an opportunity to wreak havoc on the retiree of old, since his time threshold was short. Boy, have things changed!

Today, industry downsizing has resulted in people being forced out of their jobs earlier than they expected. Companies now use terms like "right-sizing", "staying competitive" and even "eliminating waste" to justify the plans that are impacting much of the work force. Hence, the main breadwinner may be forced into retirement long before expected and may not be financially prepared to support his spouse and himself.

The following are cases of typical working-class people, depicting how retirement has evolved over the years. The examples below describe their lives and how their lifestyles impacted their retirement. We will examine the following generations:

- Grandpa's Generation—Born before WWII
- Dad's Generation—The so-called "Baby Boomers", born after WWII
- The Younger "Now" Generation—Children of the baby boomers

1.1 The Older Generation—Born Before World War II – Grandpa's Generation.

Back in Grandpa's day (and in Dad's early days) many companies took care of financing their employees' retirement with non-contributory pensions. The employer paid 100% of these benefits. The worker and spouse would typically receive a monthly payment for life after reaching retirement at age 65. The average worker in those days worked for one or, at most, two companies in his lifetime. At retirement the employee received a golden handshake, maybe a gold watch, and a pension to help support the employee and spouse for the rest of their lives. The worker typically saved very little additional money for retirement since just making everyday ends meet was a challenge.

Grandpa retired with Social Security as well as a pension and was able to live off these until the day he died, which typically was less than 10 years after retiring. However, Grandma frequently lived many years longer since she tended to be younger and also had a longer life expectancy. With the loss of part of her deceased husband's pension and his Social Security she normally lived poorly. She couldn't afford to travel, sat around knitting, listening to the radio and watching television. In many cases she couldn't even afford to live alone, forcing her to move in with relatives, often feeling like little more than a burden.

The Baileys

John Bailey, a mechanic, turned 65 years of age a few years ago and was forced to retire from his employer of 35 years. Note that the laws have since changed so that forced retirement due to age is no longer an acceptable practice. John was eligible for a company pension that paid him $900 per month and he also received Social Security that paid him an additional $1,400 per month. His wife Edna was a homemaker and never earned a paycheck. She was 6 years younger than John, and had to wait until she turned 62 to be eligible for Social Security. She now receives her own Social Security check of $400 per month.

They had managed to save $20,000 over the years and had no debt other than a car payment, which will be paid off in another year. They paid off their home mortgage some years ago and now proudly own their $125,000 home outright. They live in the same town as their children and grandchildren and hardly ever take an expensive vacation. John will likely live another few years and Edna an additional 10 years without John, leaving her to manage finances on her own.

Early on in their retirement years, they found that their income, consisting of John's pension and their Social Security checks, enabled them to continue to live as they did prior to John's retirement. In recent years this income seems inadequate to cover all their expenses as inflation has increased all their costs. They have quickly used up the $20,000 nest egg. Now that their modest savings are gone they must consider selling their home for the cash equity and moving into an apartment. Other alternatives include taking out a home equity loan or taking out a reverse mortgage that will allow them to live in their home but eventually relinquish ownership.

The Thompsons

Bob Thompson, a postal clerk, was even less prepared than John Bailey. His pension amounts to $700 per month and he has only $3,000 in savings. His home is worth $60,000 and needs many repairs, including upgrading of the heating system and plumbing, a new roof, and replacement windows. Bob and his wife Gladys have credit card debts totaling $13,000 and car payments that will last another year. Bob and Gladys are now both receiving Social Security. Bob receives $1,100 while Gladys receives $400 as a non-working spouse. Social Security combined with Bob's pension is not nearly enough to allow them to enjoy their golden years.

Bob and Gladys aren't able to afford to go on any vacations or do much of anything that is costly. Their "luxuries" are limited to going to the movies once a month. They drive a beat up old car and struggle through the car maintenance costs. Bob has to ask friends to help him out by performing house and car repairs. The Thompsons find their meager savings were gone after their first year of retirement. Now, even weekly food shopping feels like a drain on their funds. They have already applied for food stamps and other assistance from the State.

Bob can't imagine where he went wrong. He did what was expected of him and now he has to practically beg for money. The realization has finally hit that Bob couldn't actually afford to retire. He needs to work at least part-time and could consider full-time employment if not for his ailing back. To add insult to injury, the Thompsons now find themselves hounded by bill collectors and are considering moving in with their children.

1.2 The Baby Boomers—Those Born Soon After WW II.—Dad's Generation.

Dad had a number of opportunities to change jobs during his career and frequently took advantage to improve his position and increase his salary. Some of his employers offered pension plans and some did not. By changing jobs frequently, his pensions were substantially reduced as compared to a pension earned when staying with one company. This is because a pension is typically "frozen" based on the last salary and the number of years one served the company before leaving. Unlike working for a single employer, the worker changing jobs could not depend on advancing seniority as well as increasing salary to build his future pension. Late in his career, Dad found that the corporate attitude towards pensions was changing as companies were starting to eliminate pension plans. Soon companies stopped providing pensions to new employees and also stopped allowing pension accumulation for existing employees.

Meanwhile, medical science has provided people with "wonder drugs" to ward off many deadly diseases as well as new tools to diagnose disease early. Perhaps the greatest positive health impact was the realization that smoking was a deadly killer. The baby boomer was probably exposed to smoking early in life before the dangers were well known but had the opportunity to quit before too many years. The net result was a major increase in life expectancy for this group. A retiring couple might now live in retirement for up to 30 years.

The baby boomer generation was not schooled in the need to save for retirement. With 30 or more years of inflation to eat away at the retirement nest egg, there was a savings gap that is only being recognized now. Basically, Dad learned too late that he needed to set aside a very significant sum of money to support his intended retirement lifestyle of leisure activities like golf, fishing, and hunting as well as his thirst for travel.

When the baby boom generation was in their 30s, the government recognized the need for people to supplement their pensions and save for the number of years they will be living in retirement. Tax-deferred Individual Retirement Accounts (IRAs) were made available to all individuals and tax-deferred accounts (called 401(k)s) were created for the work place. Each of these allowed the individual to put aside many thousands of dollars each year into personally owned and managed accounts while also saving a substantial amount of tax dollars. This provided an opportunity to invest and grow the money while the government continued to defer the taxes on such sums until withdrawn at retirement.

Frequently company sponsored 401(k) plans have the added inducement of the company matching a portion of the employees investments. Hence, this is an excellent way for employees to save since they are getting money (read FREE money) from the employer as well as temporarily saving the taxes on their contributions and allowing that to grow as well. Over time these accounts can build very substantially if contributions continue and if the funds are left in the plan.

The problem is that many people live beyond their means and as such feel that they have "better things" to do with their money. They buy large houses and expensive cars, take nice vacations, pay college tuition(s), etc. The need to save for retirement often seems so pointless since it is so far in the future. The net effect is that many employees do not take advantage of these opportunities to save. The boomers live much better than their parents and have no compunction about spending on luxuries and other non-essentials. Saving for a "rainy day" is often not even considered.

The Williams

Jack Williams was born in 1947. He obtained a college degree in engineering and married his college sweetheart, June, who had a college degree in accounting. June is the same age as Jack. Together they raised three children. They sent two of their children to state universities and one to Yale.

Jack changed engineering positions a number of times and found that two of the positions offered modest pensions. June also worked for a few years, but discontinued her career to raise her children returning later to part-time work. She never had a pension plan. Jack and June are now both eligible for Social Security. They own a $400,000 house with a $200,000 mortgage. Unfortunately, neither of them contributed much to IRAs since they had plenty of bills to pay including a hefty mortgage, annual vacations, college tuition, luxury car payments, etc. Recognizing that they would be short of retirement funds, they only started to contribute to their 401(k)s and IRAs after reaching their late 40s. They now have accumulated $110,000 through their 401(k)s and IRAs and have little additional savings. They owe $20,000 in credit card debt and have two monthly car payments.

When they retire they will receive a total of $2,600/month from Social Security and $1,300/month from Jack's pensions. The combined $47,000 per year of income will come close to meeting their retirement needs and they will only need to pull out a small amount of their IRA money to make ends meet. They plan to travel extensively once they retire and so will spend down their nest egg at an additional $25,000 per year rate to finance their travel plans and other retirement activities that they had always dreamed of doing. Over the many years of their retirement, inflation will eat away at the purchasing power of Jack's pensions making it somewhat of a struggle to make ends meet.

Imagine their surprise when it dawns on them that Jack will actually need to find part-time work to supplement his income so that they can live their retirement years as they intended. Jack will have to work out of town since there are no local engineering jobs available. He will once again be on the road at the age of 68. June will not need to work since Jack's income will be sufficient to bridge the gap. But the good life will likely be slightly out of their reach.

The Sawyers

Joe and Cheryl Sawyer are both white-collar workers. Joe is a bookkeeper and his wife, Cheryl, is an administrative assistant. At their peak they have earned $75,000 per year between them. They do not have college degrees and have saved very little for their retirement outside of their 401(k) plans. They are not eligible for any corporate pensions but are both eligible for Social Security payments which will total $2,300 per month. They saved a good percentage of their income through their employers' 401(k) plans that now total $100,000. They own their own home valued at $200,000. They owe $10,000 on their credit cards and still have a car payment on one of their cars.

The Sawyers were always careful about their spending habits and do not live extravagantly. Because of this they will be able to come close to living on their Social Security payments alone. But they will fall short. They will quickly drain their 401(k) accounts unless they keep working into their retirement years. They will have a choice. Either Joe will need to keep working full-time until he reaches age 70 or both Joe and Cheryl will need to work part-time. Their white-collar backgrounds will probably make it easy for them to find employment in their later years. Since they have both worked their whole lives, continuing to work will seem perfectly natural to them.

The Franklins

Ted and Lynne Franklin have been dedicated hard-working people most of their lives. They worked six days a week, stayed late working evenings, and seldom took vacation. They also lived modestly, driving inexpensive cars and avoiding expensive restaurants. They have no children.

Ted is a maintenance worker with no established pension and Lynne works for a major corporation in an administrative role. Lynne has a corporate pension that will pay her $700/month when she reaches age 65. They are both eligible for Social Security payments that will total $3,300/month. Always looking ahead, they saved much of their income over the years in 401(k) plans as well as their own personal IRA savings accounts since they had little time or desire to spend much money. They started to save when they were in their early 30s and carefully invested their nest egg with an excellent investment advisor. They sat back and watched their retirement nest egg grow. They will retire with accumulated wealth of more than $1,000,000.

Investing their $1,000,000 to grow at only 7% per year coupled with their Social Security and pension income will allow them to have an enjoyable and fulfilling retirement. Now they will be in the position to enjoy the luxuries and activities that they had only thought about doing but never had the time. They can thank their austere living conditions that made all this possible. Although the Franklins didn't have professional careers, they are a true success story. Unfortunately, stories like theirs are few and far between. But there are many lessons to be learned from them.

What Happened to the Baby Boom Generation?

The baby boomers were the first generation raised to expect the good life. Perhaps the sacrifices of their parents paved the way. They were also the first to benefit from government programs like tax-deferred accounts. The boomers might have started their careers with companies that offered excellent pensions and profit sharing plans but, in too many cases, will not finish their careers with these entitlements intact. Even Social Security is challenged to keep up with the promises made to the taxpayers. Social Security may need to increase the age to receive full benefits and may also need to tax the benefits more in the future.

Many baby boomers had excellent company savings plans like 401(k) plans and had the opportunity to also put money away on their own via tax deferred IRAs as well as personal savings and investments. Although it seems as though they should do fine in retirement, many will not. The vast majority of this group did not feel compelled, or recognize the need, to start saving for retirement until they reached their fifties. Now, it is very difficult for many, especially those with modest salaries, to play catch-up in time for retirement. Those who can't (or won't) learn to live modestly will need to continue working well into retirement. The baby boomers have significantly longer life expectancies than past generations. This will result in many more years in retirement and a greater need to accumulate wealth for these years.

A major expense associated with living longer is the increasing cost of staying healthy. Fidelity Investments estimates that a retired 65 year-old couple, in good health, would need on average $215,000 to cover medical costs in retirement. These costs include Medicare premiums, supplementary insurance, prescription drug costs, non-covered services, co-payments and deductibles. Additional sums will be required for over-the-counter medicines, dental work, or long term care insurance premiums. There are some who claim that $215,000 underestimates the basic medical cost and that it is likely to be in excess of $300,000 per couple. If the retirees have serious health issues, live in an expensive area, or outlive their life expectancy, they can expect to pay even more.

Clearly, the majority of baby boomers are not well prepared for retirement. They will try to compensate in some manner. So what will they do?

- Will they learn to live much more modestly? – It will be very difficult for people to change their lifestyles after so many years.
- Will they keep working well beyond retirement years? – While there is already some indication that this is already happening, finding jobs after age 65 can be difficult. Many employers would rather hire younger workers, viewing older workers as too expensive and resistant to new technologies.
- Will they take major risks in trying to grow their assets? Will they invest in risky stocks and other investments? Will they just start gambling? And if so, what will happen if/when they lose?

The jury is out on how this will all play out.

1.3 The Now Generation—Children of the Baby Boomers—Presently in their late 30s through early 50s.

Dad learned too late that he needed to set aside a very significant sum of money to support his intended retirement lifestyle. It may be too late for Dad to react to these needs, but it is not too late for the next generation to prepare themselves. To do so, it will be necessary to change old spending habits and develop new ones in order to make the transition from a "live-for-the-moment" generation to an austere, forward-thinking, and planning generation.

But the question remains to be answered: Has this generation gotten the message? The baby boomer generation has, more-or-less, finally gotten the message about the need to control their spending in order to save for the future. However, many in that generation are still in denial. Now it is necessary for the message to be passed down to the next generation. So far the Now Generation doesn't seem to be getting the message. They are still living in a material world with little thought of the future and without the discipline and self-control needed to prepare for their retirement years.

The Mitchells

Jason Mitchell is 40 years old. His salary as a salesman is $80,000/year. He has three daughters and a wife Deborah, also 40, who works as a dental hygienist earning $25,000/year. Jason has a 401(k) plan at work and no pension. Deborah has neither of these. The Mitchells live in a large five-bedroom house, valued at $350,000, with a $2,700 monthly mortgage. They presently have $150,000 in equity in the house. The big old house always seems to need repairs – a new roof, new windows, a replacement driveway, new appliances, and other unexpected needs that go with an aging house.

They drive two heavily financed cars. They go on nice vacations every year, flying the whole gang to Europe, Disney World or some other exciting, and costly, location. The Mitchells can't make ends meet. They borrow heavily on their credit cards and at the end of the year have no savings beyond Jason's 401(k). He typically puts away enough money (6%) to get the employers matching funds (3%). At least they are prudent enough to take advantage of a free company match.

When the Mitchells retire in 20+ years, they will have saved very little but will have Jason's 401(k) that should be worth roughly $400,000. The equity in their house will likely grow to about $350,000. They intend to become snowbirds, purchasing a "winter condo" in Arizona to get away from the cold winter weather of the Midwest. It will cost them $200,000 in cash to make the condo purchase, which may be something they can ill afford. Yet, the

Mitchells will still make the purchase because they really want the condo and feel they are entitled to it. They may elect to downsize from their house to a condo or town house as they reach retirement. They want a luxury condo and will trade in their home equity for the condo. This will leave them without much of a nest egg to live on.

Their Social Security income of roughly $2,900 per month will be inadequate for them to take full advantage of their golden years. They will recognize that Jason will need to work at least 2 or 3 extra years to build up his 401(k) and their savings as well as reduce their costs in retirement. Otherwise they will be struggling through their retirement years and will spend down their equity faster than they should in an effort to maintain their life style. Since they will need to live off their nest egg for close to 30 years, the ravages of inflation will impact them and add to their frustration.

The Millers

Horace Miller is 42 years old. He works as a welder in a machine shop earning $50,000 per year plus overtime. His wife, Candy is 40 years old. She is an assistant teacher at the local grade school and earns an additional $12,000 each year. They have two children who go to the local public schools.

Neither Horace nor Candy has a 401(k) plan at work. Their house is worth $100,000 and they have paid off only a small portion of their mortgage. They have difficulty saving money and have a total bank checking account of $2,000. Their credit card debt is $19,000 and they still have two years of car payments.

They have trouble making ends meet each month and rely on their credit card to keep them whole for the month. They try to minimize their expenses but often find the needs of their family including mortgage payments, utility bills, braces for their children's teeth, car payments, clothing for school, and miscellaneous expenses just keep coming up. There is no money available to take expensive vacations. A typical vacation for them is a week camping at a state park.

When they retire at age 65 they will receive Social Security payments and hopefully have their house paid off by then. They will be living hand-to-mouth and at least one of them will need to work past the age of retirement just to keep up with their expenses. They may both end up working at the local supermarket to make ends meet.

Sadly enough, they will probably spend their golden years sitting around the house and watching television, except when it's time to go and bag groceries. They will need to eventually sell their house and move into an apartment. If they have medical bills, let alone serious ones not covered by Medicare, they will be unable to pay them. They will not enjoy the longer life expectancy they can expect and could turn into a little more than a burden on their families in their later years.

The O'Learys

Paul O'Leary is a 43 year-old engineer. He earns $105,000 per year. His 41year old wife Sara is an administrator, earning $25,000 annually. They have three children who attend the local public schools. Paul and Sara grew up from poor working class families where there was never any extra money for the luxuries of life and so they have always been prudent savers. They both started IRAs when they were in their mid thirties, putting away the maximum amount allowed. Paul set up a 401(k) through his company and again contributed the maximum amount. He also received his company's matching 3% share. He has no pension or profit sharing plans. Paul and Sara live in a $300,000 home and have a $150,000 mortgage they can readily afford from their combined salaries.

The O'Learys typically enjoy a nice one-week vacation every year which could be a trip to Florida or California or renting a cabin at a lake or at the ocean side. Their second annual vacation consists of day trips to just have fun. Their children's daily activities are limited, and so do not run up much expense. There's dancing school for their daughter and their sons' activities are primarily sports oriented, which are not very costly. The O'Learys are very frugal and managed to save an additional $5,000 each year that they put into a joint investment account. Both the IRA and 401(k) coupled with their personal savings will likely approach $2,000,000 by the time Paul is 65 years old. By that time, they will have their mortgage paid off and their home will be worth another $400,000.

The O'Leary's will be able to live their retirement years in most any way they choose. Conservatively investing their $2,000,000 nest egg at 5%

will provide $100,000 per year of income to add to the $30,000 per year they will get from Social Security. Their austere lifestyle and accumulated savings, combined with Social Security, should make their golden years a true joy. They will also be in position to help their children purchase their first homes and jump start businesses if needed. Their thrifty living has paid off for them.

1.4 Why Can't They All be Successful?

Some of our case histories are real success stories. But most are not. The stories mirror the degree of (or lack of) preparation we find in the lives of today's adults. The vast majority of future retirees will be somewhat disappointed in their retirement lifestyles. But they could all have more fulfilling retirements with proper planning.

Some couples are blessed with unique situations that few can hope to achieve. Not everyone can become a junior executive or own a good moneymaking enterprise that can continue to produce cash after retirement. The O'Leary's, on the other hand, did not have a unique situation. Instead, they relied on austere living and good planning to put them in an enviable retirement situation. Most retirees **can** be the O'Leary's.

Jason and Mary Mitchell collectively earned over $100,000 each year, which over 30 years would total in excess of $3,000,000. If they could have invested only 10% of their income for 25 years they would have close to $750,000 to live on at age 65.

Horace and Candy Miller were far from financially blessed. Nevertheless, if they could have put aside $3,000 per year for 30 years they would also have quite a nest egg. Investing that money at 10% return would have left them with more than $250,000. This sum coupled with Social Security could lead to a fine retirement for the couple. Unfortunately they didn't know how to take control of their finances and will likely have to consider working for the majority of their retirement years.

There was sufficient income available for most of our families. They could have been prepared for retirement. But they were not. Why not? All excuses aside, the real reason is that they simply didn't know how to prepare for their retirement years. All that was needed was a proper road map and enough motivation to change their habits. ***The Five Dollar Cup of Coffee is Ruining My Retirement*** will provide the path forward for developing the discipline and know-how to make the retirement years all they can be.

Chapter 2

What Changed?

Financial planning for retirement in Dad's day and age could be described in three words: pension, Social Security, and savings. These are sometimes known as the "three-legged stool". Mom and Dad could count on funding most of their retirement through their Social Security and pension without having to worry about saving very much additional money.

Most employers provided pensions for their workers who frequently were not even aware how critical this was to their future financial health. Social Security, provided by the government, and financed by both the worker and employer was also automatic. In many cases the worker was hardly aware of what was being put aside for him. Then, if the employee was astute enough to save a few additional dollars along the way, the path to retirement was sweetened, allowing him to spend his few retirement years without worry.

With the three-legged stool of pension-Social Security-savings, and the relatively short number of retirement years, the importance of savings was not critical. So what changed?—Lots of things. Much of the financial burden and risk of retirement planning now falls upon the worker. There are very few corporate sponsored guarantees. Unfortunately, today's worker is frequently unaware of how to fend for himself financially. Many are just not financially literate. Even the highly educated person is not much better. The future retiree does not have a good model to follow since past generations did not need to save for the long haul ahead.

2.1 Pensions

Pensions are very quickly becoming extinct. Today, only one in five U.S. workers still has a traditional pension plan. How did this change come about?

Originally, corporations recognized that the cost of replacing a knowledgeable, well-trained worker was quite high. Hence pensions were created and financed by employers as a fringe benefit designed to attract and keep quality workers. The pension was a promise to pay the worker later—many years later—in exchange for being a valued employee and remaining with the company. This promise was considered a sound business decision that positively impacted the profitability of the company. The long-term impact pensions had on the company's bottom line was often obscured by creative accounting techniques. It was not always obvious that the long-term promise would even impact the company's profitability at all. Now modern accounting procedures require that companies show the pension commitment as a business expense, thereby directly impacting profitability.

In the past, the shorter life expectancy of the worker generally resulted in pension payments lasting only five to ten years after retirement. Hence, the pension appeared to be a wise business agreement for both the worker and the company. Life expectancies are now expanding quickly, bringing the cost of pensions up along with them. Retirees are now living in retirement for 20-30 years. This makes pensions much more expensive and, in turn, less cost-effective to businesses that dole out these extended payments.

There has been a steady decline in traditional pensions over the past 20 years. But the downward trend is now accelerating at a feverish pitch. More than 2/3 of employers that once offered traditional pensions have closed their plans to new hires or have frozen, or plan to freeze, their plans for all employees. This trend is no longer confined to troubled industries like the airlines, steel, or automotive but now involves healthy growing industries as well.

The value of the individual worker to the employer has changed significantly in three major ways:

- Modern technology has made the experience of the individual worker less valuable and at times even made the experienced worker obsolete.
- Many jobs are now exported to distant lands where much lower wages are paid for the same work.
- The overall fringe benefit costs tend to grow with each year the employee stays on. This is now seen as a significant burden to the company's profitability.

The bottom line seems to be that the worker is no longer valued as much as in past years and is sometimes even viewed as expendable. In too many cases, employers have come to believe that workers do not become more valuable with seniority, but instead just become more expensive.

Large, well-known Fortune 500 blue-chip companies, who in earlier years were paternalistic toward their employees, now feel pressured to reduce costs in order to stay competitive. They are engineering cutbacks in order to protect the company's solvency that, in theory, should also protect the remaining jobs. It is no longer unusual to offer "early-out packages" which represent a payoff of a sum of money to aging workers in order to induce them to retire sooner. Sometimes there is even an implied threat that the worker could be forced out anyway and lose many of the inducements if they don't accept early retirement. Full-scale layoffs, with modest severance penalty to the employer, are utilized in more severe cases to reduce staffing. Layoffs end any further accumulation of the individual's pension benefits. The younger worker is anxious to fill these jobs, and is willing to accept them without a pension. Besides, to the younger worker there is less thought of looking ahead the many years to their retirement benefits.

Many companies, such as the airlines and automotive industries, over the years succumbed to union pressure and promised very lucrative pension plans to employees in order to avoid labor strife and also retain their best workers. The pension plans, in many cases, were managed so poorly that the plans were no longer solvent. This represented a big loss to the business or its employees. There is fear that some of these companies will have to go into bankruptcy and be unable to meet their pension obligations. The Federal Government, which guarantees pension funds for individuals, is sometimes left to pick up the pieces and take over the poorly funded pension funds as best they can. The government, however, can only guarantee to meet minimal pension criteria and so some employees may get far less than their pension programs promised.

Yet, all is not lost, as things tend to change with time. Future population aging trends suggest a possible silver lining. There is a projected shortage of skilled workers in certain industries once the baby boom generation begins retiring in great numbers. This could greatly improve opportunities for the aging worker although it is unclear what impact technology will have on the work force. It is conceivable that corporate America will once more recognize that aging employees are indeed valuable and take measures to keep these skilled workers in the workforce beyond retirement. The hope is that those able, and needing to work, will stay in the work force and compensate for the loss of retiring employees. But, there is no guarantee that this will all work out smoothly.

2.2 Social Security

Make no mistake about it, Social Security will be there for future retirees. However, the Social Security program is under extreme financial pressure. The government recognizes this but is caught up in numerous political stalemates in trying to resolve the impending shortfall of funds. Our politicians (both parties) are presently falling all over themselves to claim that Social Security is sacred and will not be subject to any cuts. The politicians promise to do something to keep the system solvent indefinitely but very little has been accomplished thus far.

Retirees as well as aging baby boomers form a massive voting block supported by the American Association of Retired Persons (AARP). Retirees have a history of actually going out and voting, tending to magnify the political pressure this group represents. Most politicians recognize that it would be political suicide to make any public statements against this powerful group.

Eventually our elected officials will make the hard decisions and correct the financial problem. But who knows when? There is still a lot of work to be done. But, as always, there is hope.

How did this happen? The Social Security System was designed in the 1930's when approximately twenty workers paid into the system to support each retiree. There has always been great excess income from Social Security that the government utilized for various spending programs in an effort to control the increasing Federal budget deficit. For example, recall Al Gore's desire to create a "lockbox" for Social Security. Mr. Gore boasted that he would protect the consumer by putting Social Security money in a "lockbox" so that the funds could only be used to pay for Social Security. The snickers he received for the way he presented the concept were instrumental in costing him the 2000 election.

Unbeknown to most, Social Security is still operating with a small surplus that will disappear very soon. In fact, it is projected that by the year 2020, only 1.5 employees will be left in the work force to provide the payments needed for each retiree receiving benefits. This is far less than the original ratio of workers to retirees and sets the groundwork for an intergenerational political war to keep Social Security solvent.

Social Security will need to be adjusted in order to continue to meet the obligations the government has made to the retirees. Some of the future corrections being considered include:

- Reduced monthly benefits
- Reduced inflation adjustments (COLA's)
- Increased retirement age
- Increased taxes on Social Security
- Eliminating or reducing the benefits paid to certain "well-to-do" citizens. Since the term "well-to-do" is a relative term, it is not clear who might ultimately be affected.

It is clear that the retiree can't expect any significant enhancements in payments and may even need to live with somewhat reduced benefits. It is apparent that the employee is going to have to take more responsibility for his or her own financial future then ever before. Since according to AARP, one in three retirees will be depending on Social Security for 90% or more of their retirement income, the results will have a major impact. Nevertheless Social Security alone will be insufficient to allow them to live the retirement lifestyle they are expecting.

2.3 Savings

Savings is the third leg of the pension-Social Security-savings stool. Future retirees have extensive control of only this leg, and can therefore make critical decisions that will affect their financial future. Yet most workers do not appreciate the value of saving and tend not to take full advantage. Perhaps this is because there is no model to follow. Judgment is often clouded by the feeling that there are more immediate needs for this money, and so do not save and invest properly on their own.

Although a number of U.S. households claim to be actively saving and investing for retirement, they have not accumulated nearly enough. See the following table:

Less than $10,000 Saved	26 %
$10,000-$25,000 Saved	5 %
$25,000-$50,000 Saved	9 %
$50,000-$100,000 Saved	11 %
$100,000-$250,000 Saved	20 %
Greater than $250,000 Saved	29 %

The figures are staggering when one keeps in mind that assets well in excess of $250,000 will be required to live a comfortable retirement in the vast majority of cases. Unfortunately, few prospective retirees are even aware that they will be coming up substantially short of their retirement needs.

The government recognized some years ago that people would need to take more responsibility for their retirement. They introduced a number of tax-advantaged investment vehicles intended to induce the worker to save on his/her own. There are a few major programs that the government has pursued:

- Individual Retirement Accounts (IRAs)—aimed at the individual to save on his own.
- 401(k) accounts—company sponsored plans aimed at the inducing the individual to save by tax advantages and, in most cases, the employer matching some of the funds.
- 403(b) plans—tax-advantage plans for government employees.

These plans provide for pretax savings so that the individual can temporarily save the income tax associated with the amount deposited until such time as the funds are withdrawn (hopefully after retirement). A Roth IRA operates a little differently in that it does not allow for pre-tax contributions but permits the accumulated account to grow tax-free, with no tax impact upon withdrawal. The other vehicles, 401(k) plans and conventional IRAs are taxed upon withdrawal.

These accounts were designed to encourage saving for retirement by penalizing the individual if funds are withdrawn prior to the retirement years—before age 59 1/2. Today, according to AARP, only half of all workers have put money in employer-sponsored retirement accounts. Just 7 % of all workers contribute to their own IRAs and they've only compiled an average of only $25,000, which is not nearly enough for a comfortable, rewarding retirement. Unfortunately 29% of all households in America don't have a 401(k) plan or an IRA. What will these people do?

The government recognizes that workers sometimes need to be coerced into helping themselves and now permits businesses to automatically enroll workers in 401(k) savings plans. The employee can opt out after they are enrolled, if they so desire. But most do not. After all, it has become common knowledge that such enrollment will serve the individual well.

It is not unusual for a husband and wife to contribute separately to these accounts. The net accumulated amount can easily grow to over $1,000,000 over a number of years if couples take full advantage of the programs and start early enough. This would be quite a nest egg and would contribute nicely to their planned retirement including unforeseen expenses.

The strategy of saving will be explored in later chapters. But it is really quite simple. Don't waste your money on unnecessary items. There is no reason why someone has to drive a Mercedes when half of the cost of the overpriced vehicle can be added to your nest egg and allowed to grow over time. Saving presents the worker with an opportunity to take control of his/her own life without depending on the guarantees of others. Going beyond tax-advantaged savings, it is a good idea to save as much as possible. Keep in mind that $10,000 saved per year and invested over a 25 year time period could easily grow to $750,000.

2.4 Early Retirement by Choice?

Ten years ago the average retirement age for all U.S. workers was about 60 years of age. Recently it has risen to 62, a shift that many believe is due to the need for increased personal savings to replace traditional pensions. Recent surveys indicate that roughly 50% of people presently employed expect to work past age 65. This is primarily due to their recognition that they need to do more to finance their retirement and the growing awareness that the average worker won't be able to afford a comfortable retirement without working beyond retirement age. Unfortunately, many workers will be forced out of employment by layoffs, retirement inducements, and other factors, including technological obsolescence.

A recent survey found that roughly four out of ten recently retired workers left their jobs sooner than they wanted. This was due to a combination of health problems and job loss. Since the work force is getting healthier, the loss of their job was far and away the major cause of unplanned retirement.

2.5 What are the Real Choices?

Those lucky enough to have rich relatives or high income jobs can continue to live any way they choose. However, most of us do not fall into this group. Most people 20 to 30 years away from retirement feel they have better things to do than worry about what seems so far off into the future. Unfortunately, it sneaks up on them over time. The realization tends to hit far too late to take appropriate action.

The financial alternatives that an individual must weigh early in their career are the following:

1. Pick the right parents
2. Save until it hurts
3. Work well into retirement
4. Get really lucky

Getting really lucky seems to be the path inadvertently chosen by most people. They are not wealthy, having chosen the wrong parents, and believe they're unable to save. They even decline to take advantage of government and employer sponsored benefits like IRAs and 401(k) plans.

Many of these people can be found at casinos, racetracks, and the corner store buying lottery tickets. They need to realize that they can not depend on luck. One has to create his/her own way, and that can't be done without hard work and an understanding of what needs to be done. Otherwise they will undoubtedly join the ranks of those working well into retirement.

As you read on, you will recognize that the focus of this book is to make people realize that they need to decide now, while they still have time to control the results, how they want to live in their "golden years". Remember that times have changed and you need to take control of your life.

Chapter 3

The Fruit of Your Labor—Avoid Working in Retirement

A number of very wise men have addressed the beauty of having leisure time to enjoy.

- *"The end of labor is to gain leisure"*—Aristotle
- *"The first half of life consists of the capacity to enjoy without the chance. The second half consists of the chance to enjoy without the capacity"*—Mark Twain
- *"All work and no play makes Jack a dull boy—and Jill a rich widow"*—Evan Esar
- *"Grow old along with me! The best is yet to be"*—Robert Browning
- *"Work, the thing that interferes with golf"*—Frank Dane

The early Greek philosophers thought that work was vulgar. Working, to them, signified slavery and a lack of human dignity. The Greeks and Romans relegated all activities done with the hands, under orders, or for wages to the lower-class citizens or to the slaves. Plato and Aristotle saw total leisure as the ultimate wealth. Leisure is an opportunity for humans to exercise their minds, bodies, and spirit in new, exciting and satisfying ways; in a manner that could never be satisfied in the workplace. Pursuing wealth, power, and status through work was considered voluntary slavery.

While the Greeks saw people who continued to work beyond meeting their basic needs as simply fearing freedom, we in the United States sometimes see work as an end in itself. We feel like something is missing if we can't work for a living regardless of whether we need the money or not. It's no wonder the rest of the world considers us "workaholics".

Raising a family and building a career required a commitment to do what you felt had to be done. Throughout your career you have been compelled, and hopefully well rewarded, for doing things to satisfy others. Once the children are "off on their own", and you are no longer bound to a boss, a time clock, and family responsibilities, is when you can finally be free. All of your life you have been "getting ready to live" but never felt free enough to do the things you would love to do.

The retirement years represent this opportunity for complete freedom. You now can pursue life the way you and your spouse may have dreamed. After working 40 years or more, one needs an opportunity to truly "live" and do the things he/she never could during the working years. The retired worker has the time and, hopefully, the energy to enjoy the golden retirement years.

Contrary to negative myths about retirement, in most cases retirees are happier and more satisfied than middle-aged workers. Most find retirement better than they expected. This is probably due to a combination of eliminating the negative aspects of the work environment and incorporating the positive aspects of enjoying leisure.

Some of the negatives tolerated in the work force:

- Excessive workload
- Being confined to the office or factory floor all day, especially the nice days

- Minimal opportunity for advancement
- Having to tolerate people who have no social skills
- Competition in the workplace leading to snide remarks and backstabbing
- Having to compete with others for the good pay raises
- Long daily commutes
- Being restricted to one cubicle and desk, or place on the production line for the majority of the day
- Daily pressure to meet unrealistic timelines
- Lack of support from others in the workplace
- Management-speak from supervisors instead of telling it like it is
- Long drawn out meetings where you either fought with your coworkers or struggled to stay alert
- Having to deal with workaholics who didn't respect your earned time off
- General bureaucracy, procedures, and foolish rules
- Dealing with discrimination if you are a woman or minority or just plain older than the others
- Little recognition for a job well done
- Credit taken by management for your efforts

Many people are afraid of change and the unknown. They fail to recognize the opportunity retirement presents and choose to work rather than face the unknown. They take the easy way out by continuing to work. They use terms like:

- "I'm too young to retire"
- "I'm not ready to retire"
- "I enjoy working"

About 20 years ago, the government passed legislation making a retirement age illegal. Hence there is no real way to protect the worker from falling into the "I'm too young", "I'm not ready", and "I enjoy work" traps.

Why is it that so many people feel that they need to work as long as they are physically able?

3.1 Why Do We Work?

Some people have a deeply rooted love for their work. They would perform this work even without pay. People fitting this mold should not retire until they are too old or infirm to continue. But this does not fit 99% of the work force that work to provide for their families and themselves. The only good reason for these people to work in their retirement years is to provide for living expenses. Those who have saved sufficient funds really have no good reason to work. Many people, however, continue to work because they believe that working is natural and they feel like something is missing if they don't work.

The retiree must recognize that the workplace does, in fact, fulfill some very important needs. These include:

- **Companionship and human interaction**—Most people develop relationships and friendships in the work place while spending upwards of 40 hours per week with the same people. The time spent in the workplace exceeds the time most workers spend with their own families. It also allows them little time to nurture outside relationships. It is no wonder that many workers have little or no interests or friendships outside of the workforce.
- **Structure and Order**—People need a sense of routine in their daily lives in order to feel complete. The 9 to 5 workplace environment provides this structure with normal working hours, lunch and breaks times, and regularly scheduled meetings. A feeling of purpose is created when the company requires that you be at a specific place at a given time to do a job. The soon-to-be retiree may be concerned that retirement will leave him sitting around feeling useless with no sense of urgency or purpose to his daily activities.
- **Sense of Identity and Accomplishment**—People frequently identify themselves with their workplace job. They think of themselves as an engineer or a baker or candlestick maker. Those who have little other identity beyond their job, subconsciously worry that they will somehow "cease to be" without their work place identity. In addition, despite all the frustrations, the job does provide an opportunity for accomplishment. And just about everyone needs to feel they are accomplishing something.

Every retiree will need to fulfill these basic needs once they retire. Selecting activities and developing interests and relationships that fill these basic needs best accomplish this. It is not difficult to see where activities such as playing golf or tennis, joining clubs, volunteering, taking a college course and many other extra curricular programs can be utilized to meet these needs.

So you should ask yourself "why do people work when they don't need the money?" The inescapable conclusion is that the majority does it out of ignorance or fear. They do not realize that sitting down and planning out their retirement, much like they planned out their career, will eliminate the "fear of not working" and open new doors and opportunities for fulfillment.

3.2 Selecting Leisure Activities

To develop a good balanced retirement lifestyle, you'll want to spend your time in a leisurely manner and not in a rushed, overly structured environment. Contrast this with a typical vacation. For most people this is an attempt to cram as many "leisure" activities or as much sightseeing as possible into a limited time span. Every activity is scheduled and planned in order to get the most out of the available vacation time. The net effect is that the vacation, which should reduce stress and allow for spontaneity, turns out to be a madcap rush to try to cram as much as possible into the available time. Even daily exercise, which is a great way to improve fitness and reduce stress, ends up being rushed when it must fit into a tight schedule. The net effect is adding stress to one's life, not reducing it.

Spontaneity is the key. It is difficult, if not impossible, to develop spontaneity while working a full-time job since there are so many time constraints. No full-time employee can ever develop the feeling of spontaneity that a retiree can enjoy. For the retiree, time is no longer critical. Something not done this morning or today can be done tomorrow or next week. Working part-time may seem like it will allow you to enjoy your leisure. But often the pressure of having to be somewhere at a given time can impact the freedom one has earned after toiling for so many years.

Active leisure activities generally are more fulfilling than passive activities. Active leisure pursuits include anything that mentally and/or physically totally engages the individual for a period of time. Active activities include going on a trip, riding a bike, going jogging, playing golf, painting a portrait, taking a college course, doing a crossword puzzle, or reading a novel. Passive activities include watching sporting events or (the worst example) staying glued to your television set for many hours a day. Television was an excellent outlet for those who were tired and stressed after a grueling day in the business world and just needed to sit down and relax with some mindless activity. It is not a healthy activity for the retiree. Active endeavors will improve and sustain the physical, mental, and emotional well being of the retiree. Even daydreaming, meditation, reflection, and fantasizing are more of an active pursuit than staring at the TV.

The active retirees most of us visualize are undertaking fun and challenging activities. Active leisure activities play a major role in the enjoyment of one's retirement years and help to eliminate anxiety, depression, and stress that can creep up on an aging individual. Have you noticed the retired person golfing, bowling, biking, traveling, writing the great American novel, sitting at the beach reading, or doing whatever pursuit turns them on? The retiree has the time to devote to hobbies and favorite leisure pursuits and do so with relish.

What interests and activities would make your life fulfilling and fun? If you can't answer that question, you haven't thought about it enough. Everybody has dreams and interests that they would find excitement in pursuing. With enough thought, any individual will find enough activities to fill two or three retirements.

3.3 The Magic Lists

The first list presented below (the "A" List) is composed of major leisure activities that generally tend to be very time consuming. The second list (the "B" list) is composed of activities one would only need to devote small amounts of free time to participate. Developing an activity program by judiciously combining items on list "A" with items on list "B" will produce a very fulfilling program. All you need is the desire and foresight to develop a plan and plunge in. Pursuing these activities will not only create an enriched retirement but also help fulfill the needs that were previously filled by the job. In addition it will make a person more energetic, healthier, sleep better, and generally more fun to be with.

Many of these activities won't catch your fancy. But once you understand the concept, you can make up your own personalized list.

The A List

Golf	Travel	Tennis
Bowling	Take Courses	Painting
Visit Grandchildren	Teach a Course	Learn computer skills
Join clubs	Volunteer	Write a novel
Learn a musical instrument	Learn to Cook	Locate old friends on Internet
Fix up your house	Biking	Hiking
Read Books	Become active politically	Play Pool
Swim	Read and learn good health habits	Take up photography
Care for a garden and/or lawn	Develop exercise program	Play cards or mah jong
Do crossword and/or Sudoku puzzles	Run for political office	Meditate
Start a club	Fishing	Pursue an involved hobby

The "A" List, containing more than 30 activities, are all time consuming passions that one can best enjoy with the free time that only full retirement offers. A person working 20 hours per week at a part-time job will not likely be able to participate in too many of these endeavors. You should be careful not to try to do too many of these as they will more than fill up your time and perhaps create a level of stress that defeats the purpose of your new-found leisure. Recall the short-comings of the well planned vacation and how the enjoyment dissipated with constant rushing around. It is this author's feeling that 5 to 10 of the above activities will be more than enough to make the retirement years fulfilling and sufficiently challenging.

The "B" List contains over 40 ideas that in general are not big individual time commitments. This list is, in many ways more personal, than the "A" List. Some of the ideas will probably turn you off. But you should be able to think of many activities that you've always had a passion to pursue that can be substituted for the items on the list.

The concept is to utilize the activities from your personal "B" list in conjunction with the more time consuming activities from the "A" List. The "B" list activities should be pursued on a casual basis, as time permits, to fill in the available time and provide additional spice to retirement.

The B List

Take up a simple hobby	Learn mountain climbing	Attend day baseball game
Enjoy the park	Experiment with Internet search engines	Create your own blog
Join a fraternal club	Take up guitar	Write your autobiography
Join library discussion groups	Sit on the beach	Visit old friends
Make new friends	Program an I-pod	Afternoon movies
Try activities from A List	Camping	Ride a motorcycle
Take dancing lessons	Start a diary	Watch a sunset
Try snorkeling	Act in local play	Write a play
Fly a kite	Write poetry or a song	Study the stars
Learn woodworking	Attend garage sales and flea markets	Sell things on e-bay
Collect jokes from the Internet	Get a foreign foster child	Attend the race track
Ride public transit for fun	Visit places from your past	Visit places your ancestors live in
Organize a protest group	Make a party for friends	Organize a block party
Visit different baseball stadiums	Follow sports	Learn about stocks and bonds

Ideally you should seek out the 5 or 10 items of interest from your "A" List (not the author's) and sprinkle in, over a period of time, many of the items on your personal "B" List. You are cautioned not to try to do too much too soon. Begin working your program with 2 or 3 "A" List activities and a few "B" List items that you are particularly passionate about. Then let the list grow as your time and energy level allow. Do not consider yourself a failure if you only do 1 or 2 "A" List activities in combination with 1 or 2 from the "B" List. It's OK to do less. Everybody is different.

Hopefully you will have a spouse or significant other to share your retirement years. Encourage your spouse to also create their personal "A" and "B" activities lists. You and your spouse will need to be aware of each others preferred activities. It is not necessary that the lists be identical or even similar. Most successful relationships allow each party to pursue the activities that interest each one separately. As a matter of fact it is usually <u>not</u> a good idea for a couple to participate in the same activities all the time. For instance, you might want to go biking while your spouse sleeps or reads. This is fine.

However it's a good idea to have some activities you can share with your spouse. These can be nothing more than eating at least 2 meals together each day or, if there is mutual interest, attending a movie together every few days, playing bridge, attending a college course, and planning and taking vacations together. Every couple is different so don't treat these suggestions as mandatory. Many successfully retired couples pretty much go their separate ways only eating dinner, watching the news, and going to bed together. Other couples sometimes need much more "together time" with many shared activities. Only you and your spouse can make that determination.

3.4 The Healthy Lifestyle

Good health is a critical ingredient in getting full benefit from the retirement years. As a retiree, you will usually have both the time and the opportunity to develop a healthy lifestyle. Many retirees begin their day with some type of exercise. In warmer climates they will be out walking, running, or biking early in the morning. Retirement communities offer many healthful activities including swimming and water aerobics. Health clubs generally offer special off-hours packages to attract retirees. These packages are at a reduced cost to use the facilities in mid morning to mid afternoon while non-retirees are at work.

If television, the couch, and the refrigerator are your present leisure activities you must start to make changes as soon after retirement as possible. You don't want to get trapped spending your retirement days sitting in front of the TV and snacking. That will make for a short, unhealthy retirement.

Sitting around is an easy trap to fall into. The pressures of earning a living left very little time to take care of your body or your mind. It is difficult to get adequate exercise and eat properly when one is traveling on business or rushing from appointment to appointment. The worker is so stressed out at the end of the day that exercising and eating properly are far from his mind. Most businessmen only get exercise on weekends when they work around the house to catch up with projects that went wanting all week. But even housework and painting, though better than doing nothing at all, are not really appropriate exercise. Even those working people that belong to health clubs usually find it difficult to find the time to exercise. The majority of the health clubs report that people underutilize their facilities.

You will note that many of the activities on the "A" List will help you keep physically fit. It is essential that you get off the couch and use your free time to exercise and establish cardiovascular fitness. Regular exercise will increase your metabolism and raise your energy level. It will also provide the energy to participate in more of the passive activities that will make the retirement years a true pleasure.

Researchers at Harvard University have concluded that vigorous activity for sustained periods of time is essential for physical fitness. This includes performing aerobic exercises (walking at a fast pace, riding a bike, dancing, performing aerobics, running, swimming) where one is causing the heart to beat at a significantly faster pace than normal. These activities need to be performed for at least 20 minutes at a time in order to receive significant aerobic benefits and should be performed at least 3 times each week. The reader is cautioned that after many years of inactivity, one should consult with a physician before just plunging into any aerobic activities. The doctor is unlikely to discourage you but will advise a sensible approach to get started with these activities.

Many believe that normal daily activities like walking from one office to another, doing housework, mopping the floors, washing your car, or even casually throwing a baseball around will keep you fit. This is far from the truth. You need to work up a program of aerobic activities like the ones mentioned above and perform these regularly for sustained periods of time. For the typical couch potato or workaholic who had no time to keep fit, a good way to start is by simply taking long vigorous walks. You can put on your headphones, carry a bottle of water and start off walking for ½ hour at a fast sustained pace. Make sure you are not overdoing it and getting out of breath by keeping up a conversation with a fellow walker.

Don't use excuses like it's too hot or too cold. When it's too hot just go out early in the morning before the sun rises too high in the sky. Retirees have the flexibility to do this whenever they want. If it's too cold or raining or snowing just drive to the nearest shopping mall before the crowds arrive and walk back and forth through the mall. Many malls open early for mall walkers before the stores open. But don't stop for pizza and a milk shake.

Fast food restaurants are one of the fastest growing industries in America, with more and more popping up everywhere. This growth seems to coincide with the outbreak of obesity in the United States today. Similarly adult onset diabetes also has grown to near epidemic proportions in recent years. Good eating habits are essential. The retiree seldom needs to eat on the run and can plan meals so that fat and sugar intake can be controlled along with caloric intake. Care must be taken to avoid snacking during quiet times. This book does not try to teach you how to count calories and stay away from bad foods. By now you should already know almost everything you need to know about nutrition. If not, add the study of nutrition to your "B" List.

A healthy life style will help you enjoy all the wonders retirement can give you. Don't neglect keeping yourself healthy.

3.5 Travel

Having the time to travel is probably the biggest advantage of fully retiring. You can get into your car and drive to a scenic place or even across country when you get the urge. Visit a part of the country you've never been before. The travel opportunities are endless (but very costly). Many, many workers dream of retiring and finally having the opportunity to travel to distant lands and "see the world". The retiree can take the time to experience different culture or take that long cruise to far off places like Alaska, the Greek Isles, the Bahamas, or perhaps a European River Cruise.

Having the time to visit family, grandchildren and friends is a true blessing. You can spend more time with the grandchildren and other family members.

How about taking the grandchildren on driving or camping trips? It is an experience your grandchildren will cherish all their lives. Drive to distant places rather than pay the high cost of flying and car rentals. You no longer have a work schedule impacting travel for special family functions and holidays. Did you ever want to resume relationships with old friends or relatives who you haven't seen in many years? This too is now possible.

Some elderly people no longer want to endure the cold weather. Those that live in a climate that "enjoys" the four seasons, may now find it undesirable to stay home for the winter. Many of these people tend to migrate to warmer climates with Arizona, New Mexico, and Florida very popular for retirees. Unfortunately, with their friends and relatives back home, fully relocating may not be an acceptable option. A popular solution is to go away for the winter (a concept known as "snow birding"). The decision the retiree will need to make is whether to move, become a seasonal "snow bird", or just stay put and try to tolerate the four seasons.

Alternatively, upon retirement, a person may decide to pick up totally and becoming an expatriate in places like Costa Rica which has decent medical facilities and a lower cost of living. A retiree who must still work part-time to make ends meet may not be able to take advantage of the any of these options. They will miss out on a major benefit of retirement.

3.6 Sense of Accomplishment

An employee seldom got adequate satisfaction from his job. The "satisfaction" was often limited to receiving that paycheck. They felt under-appreciated and, on occasion, were even looked down upon by managers and fellow workers. This situation seems worse in the later years of employment, when the aging worker may find himself surrounded by younger people with different interests. Now he or she finds himself an outsider. With the passing years the job sometimes becomes more and more stressful and less satisfying.

However, retirement offers a real opportunity to achieve satisfaction. Since one gets to choose the activities, they can select those activities that give them the most satisfaction. Want to fish all day? Spend the day playing 18 holes of golf? How about writing that great American novel? Take a car trip with no schedule impressed upon you? Just sit home and catch up on classic movies on a rainy day? Do you get the idea?

If you think developing a healthier and more active lifestyle is not enough, retirement allows you to pursue other avenues that will improve your self-esteem as well. You can utilize your leisure time to do something meaningful for others and become actively involved in supporting various causes that always interested you. Some examples:

- Work for a political party or candidate
- Run for office
- Join a society to improve the earth
- Become a volunteer at the local hospital
- Become a leader in your Condo Association
- Collect or help raise funds for a charity
- Become active in your religious organization

One needs to be careful that participating in causes like these doesn't become an obsession and limit the enjoyment of other activities. The best approach would be to treat a selected cause as one of the few "A" List Activities.

3.7 Should you work part-time?

Some get so much personal satisfaction from their work that they probably should never fully retire until they are no longer healthy enough to keep working. But most people will get more satisfaction out of leisure activities than they ever got from their job. The only good reason for them to work part-time is to provide the funds necessary for their living expenses. Those of you who have financial needs should consider working full-time for an extra year or two and then fully retiring rather than working part-time indefinitely. Full-time work would provide much more money and continued company benefits like health insurance, life insurance, 401(k) savings, etc.

Part-time jobs can be difficult to find. You will frequently have to settle for a job well below your level of competence. Professional people have particular difficulty adjusting to this situation. It is difficult to take orders from someone the age of your grandchildren. It can be demeaning and seldom as enjoyable as you expect a part-time job to be. Working part-time makes it difficult to establish an effective leisure program. You will find your days broken up in such a way that it will be difficult to engage in some of your chosen activities.

So, work part-time if you must. But it is far better to prepare financially so that the retirement years truly belong to you.

Chapter 4

Can You Afford to Retire?

As an employee approaches retirement age, they express concern about whether they can actually afford to fully retire. The employee is likely to reflect on where all the hard-earned money went if he finds himself <u>not</u> financially prepared to stop working. If this is the case, they will likely have to give up on, or at least delay, many of the dreams that they and their spouse had planned on. That nice trip to far away places and days casually lounging in the sun are no longer readily available to them. Nor will they be able to enjoy a full schedule of interesting and stimulating activities if they have to continue working.

How much do you need to retire? Well, like everything else the answer is "it depends". A relatively healthy couple with minimal debts, a good company pension, and a modest savings nest egg totaling close to $200,000 might have adequate funds to retire provided they live modestly. Those accustomed to spending close to $100,000 annually may need a nest egg of over $1,000,000 to enjoy their retirement years. To most folks this may sound like a fortune. However, it is important to keep in mind that it really depends on how you live.

There are many rules of thumb that one can use to get a picture of a couple's needs. At the upper extreme is a nest egg more than 10 times their annual salary (if they have no pension). This may sound like a huge sum of money. And it is! Fortunately, this conservative rule of thumb does not apply to a majority of retirees. This chapter will help you personalize your needs.

When figuring out your financial needs, it is essential that you keep in mind the following factors:

- How much monthly income in pensions and social security has been promised to you?
- How much are your assets worth, excluding your home?
- Are you willing to downsize your living quarters?
- How much money have you been spending every year?
- Are you willing to live more simply and frugally in the future?
- Do you wish to travel and enjoy a very active retirement?
- How healthy are you and your spouse?
- What is your life expectancy?
- Do you want to be generous with your children and grandchildren?
- How many years are you willing to continue to work part-time?

We will now explore the factors that will help you personalize your situation.

4.1 Life Expectancy

People who work and save their entire life would like to think that they would not run out of money after retirement. However life expectancy has been rising at such an aggressive rate that it could indeed affect the current and future lifestyles of retirees and their partners. In addition the longer life expectancy allows more time for inflation to reduce the purchasing power of your nest egg. The net effect is that a couple will need more funds then ever before to live the way they want and cover their expenses until the end of their days.

There is no secret to the fact that life expectancy has been increasing in leaps and bounds. The National Institute for Health has shown that someone born in 1952 had a life expectancy of 68.6 years. By 2002 that figure had risen to 77.3 years.

The 2005 Internal Revenue Service's Life Expectancy Chart indicates the life expectancy of a person of a specific age. A column for the average remaining years for the person of that age has been included.

Age	Life Expectancy	Remainder of Life Expectancy
51	84.3	33.3
52	84.3	32.2
53	84.4	31.4
54	84.5	30.5
55	84.6	29.6
56	84.7	28.7
57	84.9	27.9
58	85.0	27.0
59	85.1	26.1
60	85.2	25.2
61	85.4	24.4
62	85.5	23.5
63	85.7	22.7
64	85.8	21.8
65	86.0	21.0
66	86.2	20.2
67	86.4	19.4
68	86.6	18.6

The table suggests that one who retires at 60 will, on average, live for an additional 25.2 years. And the employee who retires at 65 could hope to live an additional 21.0 years. Remember that these are averages, so roughly half the retirees will outlive the table. Also keep in mind that women tend to outlive men.

For a married couple, both of which are 65 year old, the odds are great (83.7 %) that one spouse will survive beyond the age of 85. There is also a good chance (63 %) that one will live to 90. Hence it is not unreasonable to expect at least one party to be living off their assets for close to 30 years.

These projections are likely to underestimate how long people will live given the rapid advances in healthcare and nutrition as well as other medical diagnostic developments. Diseases untreatable in the past are slowly but surely coming under control as earlier detection and improved treatments are available.

These are a lot of statistics. So what do all these statistics mean to you—the ordinary worker? The good news is that you can realistically expect a long and healthier life after retirement to pursue enjoyable interests and activities. Yet, it also presents a serious financial challenge since you must plan for a much longer time-horizon than did your parents or grandparents. You might even want your financial time horizon to extend beyond your life expectancy if you plan to leave money to your children and grandchildren.

4.2 How to Estimate the Required Size of Your Nest Egg?

How much money will you need when you retire? This question is very difficult to answer. There are many rules of thumb but no set answer as everyone's situation is different and there are a number of factors like inflation that are difficult to project. This chapter will give you an idea of whether you are in a good or weak financial position for retirement.

There are many spreadsheets available over the Internet from various investment services and banks that can help you develop a good, reasonably reliable, model to address the financial preparedness question. There are also financial advisors that can review your individual situation and give you a reasonably clear answer as to whether you are in a position to retire. I urge you to check with these services to get a customized answer that fits you and your lifestyle choices. Some of the larger mutual funds provide this service free of charge. You can find them via their websites and also utilize their spreadsheets. Three of the best-known funds are Fidelity, T. Rowe Price, and Vanguard.

Try the following approach to accumulate data and prepare for these analyses as well as get a rough idea of where you stand.

Net Worth—The first step is to figure out your net worth by adding up your assets and subtracting your liabilities (debts).

Your assets include:

- Savings
- Stocks, bonds, CD's, 401(k), and IRA accounts
- Equity in your home (expected sales price minus outstanding mortgage and brokers commission)
- Other property you own such as a second home or piece of land.
- Any other liquid (easily sold) assets like boats, cars, and certain collectibles.

Then figure your debts which may include:

- Car loans
- Credit card debts
- Personal loans
- Mortgage and loans on other properties
- Future expenses assumed for family members for things like weddings or college tuition

Your net worth is the difference between your assets and debts. If your total net worth is less than $500,000 and you don't have a good pension plan or wealthy relatives, you may be challenged to completely retire without a part-time job. You might also be able to make ends meet by living frugally in retirement.

Also keep in mind that we have taken credit for the equity value of your home. You can live off the equity in your home, in order to make ends meet, in a variety of ways. Some approaches include selling the house and moving into an apartment, condominium, or town house or taking out a negative mortgage which allows you to live in the house until you die at which point the bank will sell the house to recoup their investment. You may not want to do any of these if you feel strongly about living out your retirement years in your present home and maintaining full ownership.

Retirement Cash Flow—The simplistic Planner, below, will provide you with a pretty good indication of your future financial situation. There is no adjustment for inflation but is easy to understand and will give you a quick and dirty overview of your finances.

The Planner helps you determine the difference between your after retirement monthly income and living expenses. It then compares this difference to your assets and determines if the assets appear sufficient to maintain a reasonable life style once you retire. It will give you an indication of whether you have adequate assets to support your retirement or whether you are likely to be financially challenged and need to consider delaying retirement (or plan on continuing to work part-time).

Many retirees find their monthly expenses in the range of 2/3 of their final salary after taxes but it's something that differs from family to family. Those who are very active might even spend more in retirement than while they were still in the work force.

You should track your costs for many months in order to get a good handle on your spending. These are usually found by examining your checkbook and credit card bills. Canceled checks usually give you the actual utility bills, mortgage payments, auto payments, and monthly expenses. Your credit card bills normally indicate what you have been paying for gasoline, restaurants, entertainment and groceries. If you pay for these items with cash, you will need to keep a manual record of these costs for a number of months to get a good handle on them. Remember that some of these costs will need to be adjusted to depict what your costs will be after retirement. For example your restaurant lunch expenses should go down as will your clothing costs and gasoline bills, while your leisure and vacation costs would likely increase.

Make sure you account for the costs you will incur after retirement, some of which you may not be paying for directly while working. These might include, but are not limited to, medical insurance costs, medical out-of-pocket deductibles, future car payments (or savings for auto purchases), vacation allowances, travel allowances, gifts for weddings and birthdays, home repairs, car repairs, and an allowance for other unforeseen payments. Do not forget to include some new or additional expenses you may have as a retiree such as additional travel expenses, college tuition for courses at a local community college, club activities, etc.

The retirement planner is organized, with two blank columns to give you an opportunity to account for differences you might have between your first few years of retirement and the later retirement years. This accounts for later receipt of all your benefits (Social Security, Medicare, and pension income) as well as differing expenses due to changes in lifestyle i.e. summer home, one less car, and more (or less) traveling. Will your mortgage be fully paid off sometime in the next few years? This would significantly reduce your expenses.

The Planner is also useful in that you can explore the impact of taking a larger percentage of your assets for a limited time. For example you might want to live off of a greater percentage of your assets (say 5 or 6 %) for a few years and then drop back to the more conservative 4 or 4.5 % after that.

4.3 Retirement Planner—A Snapshot in Time

		Example	1st Year	5th Year	Comments
	MONTHLY INCOME				
1	Monthly Earnings after Taxes	$0			$0 if not working or income from part-time job
2	Monthly Pensions	$2,000			
3	Social Security—Husband	$1,400			
4	Social Security—Wife	$0			
5	Income from Other Sources	$900			Interest on CDs and Savings Account or Dividends
6	Total Monthly Income	$4,300			Add items 1, 2, 3, 4, and 5
	MONTHLY COSTS				
7	Out-of-pocket monthly cash	$1,200			Includes entertainment, restaurants snacks, charitable contributions, and misc.
8	Purchased health, dental, auto, and home insurance	$1,300			Could include Medicare for one and health insurance for second person plus auto and homeowners insurance averaged per month
9	Medical bills	$200			Includes deductibles to be paid and prescriptions (averaged per month)
10	Utilities	$400			Monthly average
11	Mortgage Payment	$900			
12	Real Estate Taxes	$700			Averaged per month
13	Vacation Allowance	$500			Monthly average based on $6,000/year
14	Gifts	$300			Includes family weddings and birthday gifts
15	Car Purchases	$400			Expected monthly payment for replacing auto (or monthly allowance for cash payment)
16	Car and home repairs	$200			Misc. repairs and appliance replacements estimated
17	Total Monthly Expenses	$6,100			Total of items 7 - 16
18	MONTHLY SHORTFALL	$1,800			Total Monthly Expenses (line 17) - Total Monthly Income (line 6)
19	ANNUAL SHORTFALL	$21,600			Monthly shortfall X 12
20	TOTAL NET WORTH	$600,000			Assets - Debts
21	4% of net Worth	$24,000			Typical of 4% of assets for living expenses (conservative)
22	NET ANNUAL CASH FLOW	$2,400			Line 21 - Line 19

If your monthly income after retirement, as shown in line 6, will be larger than your monthly expenses shown in line 17, you are likely ready to fully retire without working at all. If 4% of your assets are adequate to cover your annual shortfall, you are also ready to retire without needing to continue working. You will develop a positive number in the last row (line 22) of the Planner in both these cases. However a slightly negative number does not necessarily mean that you can't retire successfully. A more detailed professional financial analysis will be needed to better answer the question.

The retiring couple has the opportunity of reducing their monthly costs in a variety of ways. They should start by closely watching their pennies to control their expenses. They could also reduce many of their expenses such as limiting their vacations, reduce their auto budget, limit gifts, etc. Also keep in mind that the 4% of net worth used to determine allowable cash flow is a conservative estimate. If one needs to extract a little more, say 4½ %, it is likely to work out all right provided the retiree watches expenses very closely.

4.4 Suppose You Can't Afford to Retire

There are a number of adjustments you may want to consider if the Planner doesn't come out the way you want. There is very little flexibility on the income side of the worksheet. The only option is continuing to work. However there is much that you can do to alter your expenses on the bottom half, of the Planner. Very few of these numbers are really set in concrete. You might want to consider the impact of some of the following:

a) Out of pocket monthly cash (line 7)—This category is generally intended for essential purchases like food and gasoline. But a number of non-essential items inevitably fall into this category like entertainment, restaurant meals, non-essential driving with associated tolls and gasoline cost, etc. We will focus more completely on some of the questionable money drainers in future chapters. For now let it suffice to say that the out-of-pocket monthly cash expenses can be reduced significantly in most cases.

b) Purchased health, auto, home, and dental insurance (line 8)—These items are essential. Nobody should leave them self without insurance coverage since a major incident or illness could bankrupt almost anybody. However, keep in mind that due to Medicare, the cost of purchased health insurance will drop quite a bit when you both reach age 65.

c) Medical bills (line 9)—The main control you have over your medical bills is to stay healthy. This includes exercise, healthy habits, and weight control.

d) Utility Costs (line 10)—Make sure you consider future increases in energy costs. Hopefully your home is reasonably energy efficient. Downsizing into a condo or apartment will likely reduce utility bills.
e) Mortgage payments (line 11)—If you still have a number of years left on your mortgage, you should consider refinancing if interest rates drop. Are you ready to downsize to reduce your mortgage payments? Think about it.
f) Real estate taxes (line 12)—There isn't much you can do with this but move or downsize.
g) Vacation allowance (line 13)—How about fewer trips? Do you want to trade off expensive vacations in order to make the plunge into full-time retirement?
h) Gifts (line 14)—Have you been too generous with your children and grandchildren in the past? How important is this to you? Many retirees are not expected to be very generous.
i) Car purchases (line 15)—Do you really need two cars once you are retired? How about a smaller, less expensive, energy efficient car that will also reduce your out-of-pocket expenses.
j) Car and home repairs (line 16)—Generally downsizing will greatly reduce, or eliminate, home repair costs. The larger the car, the more expensive to repair. Many low mileage foreign cars tend to have fine maintenance records.

Everybody should consider the changes suggested here. These ideas are not only for those who can't afford to retire but also of value to those who can. Improving your cash flow by taking some of these actions will mean that you draw down your assets much more slowly and can enjoy more luxuries along the way. This would also provide an extra degree of safety as far as outliving your money as well as allow you to leave more for your heirs.

However, if you still can't turn the net annual cash flow (line 22) positive after considering all the suggested adjustments, you should indeed expect to work full-time for another couple of years or face working part-time for an indefinite period.

The Planner is designed for people approaching retirement age. At this time, it is very difficult to make enough of an impact on their assets or net worth. Of course it would have been better to build more equity in the years prior to retirement. But nobody can turn back the clock. Never believe the saying that it's too late to change. It's never too late to modify your spending habits to gain some degree of control over your golden years. Making these changes will at least minimize the number of additional years you need to work and will also enable you to develop the habits to make your retirement dollars go further.

Subsequent chapters in this book will provide detailed ideas for reducing your expenses and building your assets to enhance your chances for an exciting and fulfilling retirement.

Chapter 5

Turning it All Around

- Live beneath your means and the future will be good
- The road to financial ruin is paved with plastic
- When you're 20, it sounds like retirement is light-years away. Then you wake up one morning and you're in your 40's and life is moving like a freight train
- Then you're over 55 and your retirement years are set and it's too late to change direction substantially

Have you saved very little so far and have nothing to show for it but debts and credit card bills? Did the calculations you performed in Chapter 4 indicate that you are not on the right path to retirement? Well, believe it or not you have plenty of company. Most of our readers are in the same situation. But, there is hope so do not despair. Just recognize that you need to make changes in your lifestyle and follow some of the guidelines we will present.

If you are supporting a family on a minimum wage income, you have a genuine problem and there is genuinely little you can do to save a penny. You undoubtedly have your hands full just managing to feed your family and pay the rent. This book will help the many families who have a growing wage but their spending habits make it virtually impossible for them to make ends meet, let alone have money left over to save for their later years. All that is really needed is an attitude adjustment. The time to act is now. The following pages will provide insight and point you in the right direction. But the work is up to you.

The main question you must ask yourself: "Is it worth changing my spending habits in order to enjoy my retirement years?" If the commitment and desire aren't there you will not succeed. Just remember what seems unimportant to you now, when you have many years until retirement will seem important as you get closer. People who haven't saved for the future after 20-30 years in the work force have some behavioral issues to change. Changing a mind-set is the critical element for success. In a severe case you may need an experienced psychologist or a good life coach who specializes in retirement and money issues to help you to see the light. But don't give up too soon. Most people can change once they understand the problem and then recognize the steps they need to take to succeed. The key is to start living beneath your means not above it. You'll be surprised to see that just a few changes in your approach to spending will put you on your way.

Some believe that the secret to preparing for your "golden years" is to deprive, deprive, deprive, and when you finish depriving yourself, deprive yourself some more. But this is really overstated. You just need to recognize what you spend every day and it's impact on your savings. The secret is to develop a budget-driven lifestyle with minimal waste. You will need to eliminate certain luxuries that you've taken for granted over the years but hardly recognize as luxuries. You will have to alter your mind-set to see things in this way. Of course it's tough to recognize your "normal" daily expenditures as luxuries, especially once you have gotten used to eating out in restaurants, having wine with dinner, buying a daily latte, or going to the theater regularly. If you keep in mind that past generations lived well enough without relying on these luxuries, it becomes apparent that we truly can gain control of our budgets and, therefore, our destiny if only we would exercise restraint.

By now you probably have guessed what you will need to really focus on. Very simply stated—**REDUCING YOUR SPENDING!**

5.1 Getting into Debt

High school and college graduates are generally sent into the world with a decent education but little comprehension of managing their own money. Up to this time they might have worked part-time for pocket spending money or had no job at all. They had very little cash and so pretty much spent every penny they could get their hands on. Even though these graduates may be prepared to hold steady jobs and start their careers, they're not at all prepared to handle their own finances. After all saving for the future is the farthest thing from their eager minds when they enter adulthood and start to work full-time?

New graduates and the majority of adults typically find their mailboxes stuffed with credit card applications from every bank and financial institute in the land (or so it seems). It is no wonder that today's young people (and some not so young) think of credit-card debt as "normal"—just like having a mortgage or auto loan. In fact the credit card interest that the institutions make so easy for you to carry from month-to-month should be looked upon as money thrown to the dogs like very expensive scraps under the table. The credit card companies are "generous" enough to maintain, or even raise, your credit limit as long as the lowest required payment is made every month. They make a fortune off of the 25 %+/− interest rates they charge. They also are now giving cash back rebates of 3 % to 5 % as an inducement for you to charge every-day essentials like groceries and gasoline that were typically purchased with out-of-pocket money in the past.

Credit cards in general sure make it easy for people to spend money they don't have on items they can't afford and in many, many, cases don't even need. The average household in the United States has over $7,000 in credit card debt. Both bank and department store credit cards, along with readily available auto loans have resulted in a mountain of consumer debt. Yet Americans can't seem to get enough of this. The mantra seems to be to buy anything they'll allow you to buy. It's become an addiction and, like all addictions, those who are hooked are in denial—debt denial.

Paying the monthly minimum, roughly 2% of the balance, will keep you in debt forever. If you have a $3,000 balance at 20 % annual interest and you pay the minimum payment required indefinitely, you will have paid over $10,000 in interest charges over 40 years. That means you paid $13,000 for

$3,000 purchased. Would you buy these items for that price? Of course not! If you're carrying multiple credit card debts, add up the amount (most people underestimate), check the interest rates and recognize the need to put an end to this pattern. You can't save for retirement while you are being smothered by credit card debt.

In recent years, consumers have been draining cash from their home equity to finance their pursuit of the "good life." The growth in the value of homes (until recently) has put large sums of money in the hands of consumers who took out home equity loans. Most do not use the money to pay down their debt but to make additional purchases. This increases the chances that they will still be paying off a mortgage when they reach the retirement years. The net effect is that there will be reduced equity in their home to provide funds needed later in life.

The readily available credit of recent years has not only allowed the consumer to sink deeper into debt but has created a crisis for the financial institutions making mortgage loans to people who could hardly afford them. The banks enticed the buyers with unsustainably low initial interest rates (called teaser rates). Imagine the average Joe's surprise when the rates went up a year or so later and the mortgage payment almost doubled. He had no way of meeting these monthly payments. When home prices fell more than the down payment, the many average Joes could not even afford to sell their houses and had no choice but to declare bankruptcy thereby creating a crisis for the banks. The banking institutions then respond by tightening the requirements for loans making it more difficult for business to borrow. This immediately impacts construction and financial jobs resulting in job losses, which further aggravate the situation. Easy debt looks good but all that glitters is not gold.

5.2 Getting Out of Debt

Have you thought about getting your personal finances into shape? If not, it's time to start. If you recognize the need to shape up your financial situation, why haven't you? Do you live on excuses, excuses, and more excuses? You are not alone. Most people avoid thinking about retirement since it is decades away and they don't have any idea what to do about it. Unfortunately, this attitude typically continues until retirement is a few years away and it is too late. They find themselves in a situation where they can't afford to retire.

You need to recognize that many families manage to live on far less income than you have. How do they do this? Unfortunately some of these families just drown themselves in debt. However there are many families who get by just fine. You need to learn from those families. To eliminate your debts you must change the habits that got you into this fix in the first place. You will also need a plan to completely pay off your credit card bills. You just need to make up your mind to take the appropriate steps.

The first step is going "rock bottom" on lifestyle. This means a complete review of all the things you think you need and can't live without. Some examples of expenses and purchases worth reevaluating:

- College tuition
- New clothing
- Restaurant frequency
- Purchase of alcoholic drinks in restaurants and bars
- Purchase of dessert in restaurants
- Private schooling for children
- Wine with dinner
- Number and type of annual vacations
- Purchase of new cars
- Cable or satellite dish bills
- Buying things on E-bay
- Miscellaneous small ticket out-of-pocket money wasters

Unfortunately today's family appears to exhibit very little self-control when it comes to spending habits. Older generations seem perplexed at how modern families can spend so much on things that are far from necessary. Watch your parents' reaction to some of the luxuries you've purchased and now can't do without. In the next chapter, you will be given an in-depth analysis of typical money-wasters and some cost savings ideas.

Today, the computer and modern technology have made it easier for one to dig a financial hole. We have the "wonders" of 24-hour on-line Internet shopping as well as home TV shopping for almost anything you can think of. These were created with the impulse shopper in mind. The advertisers' motto seems to be "purchase now before you change your mind". One can stay at home and spend a month's wages without getting out of his or her slippers. Compare this with earlier generations, where the person needed to see an ad in the newspaper and/or visit the store. Before the wonder of instant credit, the consumer of old could not purchase expensive items on impulse.

Since earlier generations paid with cash, they frequently needed to go to the bank the next day, withdraw the cash, and then go to the store to make their purchase. They could not just pull out their credit card and purchase on the spot. If that burning desire to purchase was close to the weekend, there were logistical problems, such as banks being generally closed on weekends. Hence there was an opportunity for the impulse to die down. The consumer without cash in the bank would just not make the purchase. Taking out a credit application was enough to discourage the greatest impulse purchase plus it took a number of days (or weeks) for the credit application to be approved.

Today, we are so far advanced. You just swipe a credit card, without a second thought, and walk out with the product you want, whether you really need it or not. This, of course results in a high-interest loan if you don't pay off the bill in full at the end of the month. But the average Joe (or Jane) isn't about to pay off the balance when he/she can keep using the credit card and buy other "goodies" they really don't need. Now, they're simply building up more and more debt.

5.3 Avoiding Temptation

The path to success is learning to distinguish wants from needs and eliminating impulse buying completely. Everybody has a buying weakness. Learn what your temptations are. Are you an electronics geek who has to own and play with the latest electronic device? Do you crave a state of the art I-pod, cell phone, or Blackberry that you'll abandon as soon as a new version comes out?

Are you an entertainment freak—someone who has to go out to concerts, ballgames, or shows nearly every weekend? Show or sports tickets can cost a couple of hundred dollars. And don't forget that fabulous dinner before the show and drinks after the show. How about a new dress for the play? After all is said and done you have little to show for it but a big credit card bill at the end of the month. Was it really worth it?

Frequently dining out at restaurants is a "great" way to build debt and your waistline at the same time. Of course you've got to have a drink before dinner and dessert afterwards. Even with a coupon giving you the second entrée for free, you've spent between $50 and $100 on dinner for two. No need to worry. You can always charge it.

How about snacks? Can you pass an ice cream shop without stopping in for a treat? If you have your spouse and 2 kids with you, you've just spent $20, given your children a sugar high, and taken in your cholesterol allotment for the day.

How do you turn it all around? One way is to make a budget at the beginning of the month planning your discretionary spending in advance with a weekly allowance for small out-of-pocket purchases. Then, when drawn to something that is not in your budget, think of what sacrifice you will make in exchange for this indulgence. And once your out-of-pocket weekly allowance is spent, you're just out of luck for the rest of the week. Writing down your budget and carrying it with you is a helpful reminder of what you really need.

Always use a shopping list at the grocery store unless you're stopping for one or two specific items. A shopping list will keep you focused and serve as a deterrent to impulse purchases. Be especially careful at the checkout line that you don't pick up miscellaneous items (gum, candy, magazines) that are specifically put out to tempt you. Waiting on line at the grocery store with nothing to do is a sure way of finding more temptation than you need. You may find that the self checkout lane will keep you too busy scanning and bagging to get distracted into buying things you don't need.

Avoid going to the mall or any store just to spend time. Only go for a specific purchase and stay focused on that item. Leave right after making the purchase. Avoid browsing like the plague. You're just looking for trouble. When walking through a store, try to avoid handling "nice" items and certainly refrain from trying them on. Stores know all about putting out impulse items to try to coerce you into a purchase you don't plan to make. Don't fall into this trap. Where possible, carry cash and leave that credit card at home. Leaving unnecessary cash and your credit cards at home—priceless.

Find out what media tempts you the most. If television ads affect you, record your shows and fast-forward through the commercials. If you find you spend your time shopping on the home shopping network, set up your television or cable system so that this station is blocked out. If you're an Internet shopping or E-bay addict, limit Internet use to e-mail and research (or play a free game) and immediately get off the Internet when you finish. Otherwise it's easy for your mouse to click you into an expense you don't need.

There are very few major purchases that can't wait a few days. In this period you might find a less expensive alternative or realize that you can live quite well without it. When you see an expensive item you want (and can't live without) institute a cooling-off period by allowing yourself to go back and discuss the matter with your spouse or a friend. Of course you shouldn't pick the next-door neighbor with the Mercedes as a sounding board, but you do need to find someone to bounce the idea off. To justify the purchase to your spouse or friend you will first need to evaluate it yourself. This is probably the best single method of staving off impulse buying.

Consider whether you really need such an expensive item. Perhaps a much less costly one will be sufficient. For example, you should consider a less expensive pair of shoes (or jeans or dress) that might meet your needs adequately. Don't buy a Mercedes when a Toyota will get you to work quite nicely. But if the item doesn't fit your budget at all, try to avoid the purchase entirely.

Many domestic disputes, as well as divorces, are caused by one party's impulse buying. Often one partner recognizes the need to control spending while the other does not. The non-working partner in the relationship is often blamed for being the free spender and having no understanding of what is affordable for the family. However the average Joe is just as often to blame for excessive spending as the average Jane. The credit card bills pile up resulting in default and daily phone calls from bill collectors. The husband and wife start blaming one another and there goes the marriage.

There is no substitute for the two pulling together to make the program work. A good relationship with meaningful give-and-take will help resist unnecessary costs. The interaction between the partners should continuously reinforce the program by coming to a consensus on what purchases to make or not make. Should we buy a sensible family car instead of a new convertible? Should we use the money saved from buying the sensible car to modernize the kitchen or the bathroom? He wants the convertible. She wants the kitchen. Better yet, do neither and save the extra money for your future. It takes a special husband-wife relationship to openly resolve situations like this. He gives up the new Lexus. She wears last year's dress along with last year's shoes to their niece's wedding.

5.4 Managing Spending—Cutting Waste

Life is always far more expensive than you would expect. Just add up the bills and your out-of-pocket costs and you will be amazed. Then compare them to your take-home pay. Ouch!!! If there's more outgo than income, well . . . you know what to do. Ignore the problem and hope it solves itself? No. Go into hibernation? No. Blame your spouse? No. Change your habits? Yes!!! Stop eating out as often and take those electronics sites off your "book-marks" list. If you need a car, buy it used, not new, to hold the payments and insurance premiums down. You could save all you need simply by cutting out the frivolous purchases in your life.

First, you need to track your expenses for a few months. Keep a daily log to keep close track of your expenditures for that day. Write down everything you spend—and I mean everything. Then determine whether the expenditure was a) necessary, b) not really necessary, or c) an extravagance you could ill afford—an outright waste of money.

"Necessary" items include things like groceries, gasoline to get to work, and medical and utility bills.

"Not really necessary" items include things like $20 DVDs and CDs, mid-day candy snacks, an ice cream from a stand, or a designer cup of coffee and donut.

An "extravagance you could ill afford" includes items like designer clothes, $100 tickets to a concert or basketball game, a pool table, or the latest electronic game player. To help you find these in your past life, just take a look in your closets, garage, and elsewhere in your home for stuff you bought and rarely use anymore. Once you recognize the money you wasted on the myriad of unused items, you will not be likely to buy any more.

There are countless ways to cut down on your expenses. The following are a few examples. We will explore these in greater depth in the next Chapter:

- Don't throw gasoline money away. Car pool to work. Don't make unnecessary trips. Try to combine the trips you need to take.
- Cut out the soda, candy bars and other empty calories from the vending machines. Most are bad for your health anyway.

- If you smoke, quit. You'll save on cigarettes, health-care costs, and life insurance (you may even save your life). And have you seen the price tag on cigarettes these days? It's enough to make anyone grasp their chest in agony.
- Don't renew any insurance policy without first shopping around with other insurance companies. Some companies will actually help find a more suitable plan for you. Utilize their expertise—that's why they exist. Consider replacing whole life plans with term insurance. Never, ever leave your family without medical insurance since unexpected medical bills can result in irreparable damage to your finances.
- Cut down on restaurants. This habit can eat up your pocket cash very quickly or build up higher monthly credit card bills. Either way, there is much to be saved.
- For enrichment and entertainment, make frequent use of your public library's offerings, including books, DVDs and music CDs that can be checked out for little or no cost. Why rent a DVD from Blockbuster for $4, when it is $1 (or free) from the public library. You'll just need to wait a few weeks to see the movie.
- Limit your special events (date nights). Don't eliminate them. Just try to save them for special occasions. You and your spouse will enjoy them even more.
- Look for inexpensive entertainment. A "cheap" night out with dinner and babysitting can easily cost over $100. A rented movie and takeout food for dinner at home with no babysitter costs—Priceless!!! How about a night at a museum or the public library for a workshop, a class, or just a visit. It's still a night out without breaking the bank. It's amazing how much you can do for little or no cost if you put your mind to it.
- Leave your charge card and debit card home and only use cash for the daily expenses that come up. Only bring your credit card when you go out for a specific purchase. This will help you live on a budget. People always spend less when they shop with cash, and they don't get stuck with interest payments.
- Cancel subscriptions to publications you don't read (also some you do read). Ditto for health-club memberships you don't use.
- Exercise on your own. You'll save plenty of money and travel time to and from the health club.
- Pass up that daily cappuccino for a regular (or free) coffee at work. So what if it doesn't taste as good.
- Take your lunch to work. You'll save plenty and eat healthier as well.

- Do you really need all those cable channels for your TV? Check the monthly cost and decide if it is really worthwhile. Who knows? Maybe the kids will do their homework instead of staring at the boob tube.

A story about a grandmother who took her 4 year-old grand-daughter Jackie to the movies for the first time, illustrates the kind of mindset that you need to develop:

Grandma took Jackie to the movies and tried to instill a sense of values in her. She informed Jackie they had a limited amount of money and would pay to get into the movies and that Jackie had a choice of the following:

1. Purchase popcorn and two sodas in the theater, and all their spending money would be gone.
2. Just see the movie without snacks and go out for slices of pizza with sodas after the movie.
3. Just see the movie and go to the grocery store to buy a whole frozen pizza, bottle of soda, and half-gallon of ice cream. Then rent another movie from the library to watch at home for the same money.

Jackie—a natural saver, it seems—chose the third option. This is what it takes to make the necessary changes in your life—a Jackie! Now if we could all just learn to think like Jackie.

5.5 Paying off Your debts.

The frivolous expenses you eliminate coupled with the pocket change you hold on to can really add up in a hurry. You must make sure the cash gets into some form of savings or investment before natural temptation sets in and you end up using the money for an evening on the town, a new dress, or a present for someone.

It should not be difficult to save over $100 each month if you follow the tips supplied in this book about controlling your spending and saving the difference. The table below illustrates how only $100/month of savings can grow, if you allow it, by the time you retire. The table is based on investing the $100 at three different growth rates.

Number of Years	7% Growth Rate	8% Growth Rate	10% Growth Rate
1	$ 1,239	$ 1,245	$ 1,257
5	$ 7,159	$ 7,348	$ 7,744
10	$ 17,308	$ 18,295	$ 20,484
15	$ 31,696	$ 34,604	$ 41,447
20	$ 52,093	$ 58,902	$ 75,937
25	$ 81,007	$ 95,103	$ 132,683

Not a bad sum of money after 25 years. Now consider the impact of saving $200 or $300 each month. You should start to see the light, now.

Your savings will probably be limited to your workplace 401(k) until you can get out of debt. Once you're out of debt it becomes much easier to accumulate wealth. You get out of debt by paying off the worst debts first. How do you know what your worst debts are? They will be the ones accruing the highest interest rate—your credit cards. Your car loans are generally at a much lower rate. Mortgage payments, are typically a much lower interest rate than the others and so do not need to be eliminated too soon, if at all. We will be addressing this further in a later chapter.

You should pay off the credit card loans beginning with the credit card that charges the highest interest rate. Pay the minimum on your other cards while you're paying down the highest rate card. And then one-by-one cut them up leaving a single low interest card for emergency purchases. Once you learn to control your spending, you can use a credit card for daily necessities like groceries and gasoline, and take advantage of their cash back plan, as long as you pay off the balance each month

If your credit card debts are so excessive that you will need a number of years to be able to pay them off, you will need to consolidate your debts at a lower interest rate. A low interest bank loan, or a second mortgage on your home, will allow you to benefit from much lower interest rates. But you should consider a second mortgage as a last resort since it can jeopardize your home if you are unable to change your spending habits.

If the path outlined to reduce your credit card debt seems too confusing, or out of reach, you should consider finding a credit counselor who will institute a personalized debt management program for you. Credit counseling involves helping consumers develop a budget and disciplined steady payments to clear their debt loads. Basically, the counselor plays policeman, taking your monthly income and distributing a portion to your creditors until the debts are gone. Then they close the accounts.

In summary, the path to financial independence is three pronged: reduce your spending, pay down your debts, and start saving. The key is to reduce spending. The next chapter will provide insight into specific "money wasters" that many of you fall victim to and don't even recognize as you spend yourself into the poorhouse.

Chapter 6

Stop Wasting Away Your Future

In past chapters we pointed out that more and more people are finding it impossible to retire in the lifestyle they desire. We discussed many of the reasons that it is now more difficult to fully retire and how difficult it is for retired people to make ends meet. Why is this? They had poor spending habits and simply spent too much money over the years so they did not save enough to build a comfortable nest egg.

Each and every day we all spend some money frivolously. This depletes many of the valuable dollars we will need in our later years. While some can afford to do this and still have plenty of money left for their retirement years, most people cannot. This chapter will illustrate many practical ways to reduce your spending. But these are only a few examples. You will need to "get the message" and change your habits, applying these approaches to all areas of your life. Only when you change your outlook will you be able to afford the lifestyle that many others cannot.

Now let's begin.

6.1 Giving Them the Best

Everyone wants to provide the best for their family. We feel the need to open doors for our children to all the wonderful options we never had. Some of the pricier items include preschool, private schools, training in sports, dancing schools, lessons for musical instruments, the best computer, cable service, driving lessons, a new car, and eventually the best university that your money can buy. The list goes on and on, and is likely to continue indefinitely as your children learn to rely upon you to continue supporting them. What's next—a down payment on their first house? How about starting them off in a business of their own?

It's natural that you want to do all these things for your children. But can you really afford to? Chances are that you cannot. Do you think you'd be depriving the children if you didn't provide most everything on the list? Are you really doing them a favor by spending so much of your money on making them happy? You could be smothering them with kindness that they don't need (or even appreciate). It might be better to teach your children the value of a dollar and how to earn and save their own money to purchase only what they really need and can afford. Otherwise, your basement may turn into a pile of unneeded stuff that your precious angels at one point convinced you that they couldn't live without.

Many people send their children to private school in the hopes of giving them the advantages to build a better life for themselves. However, it has been well documented that the quality of an education is directly related to the effort that the child puts in, regardless of where they go to school. In addition, being in contact with a representative cross section of children, as found in public schools, helps children grow socially in a manner that generally couldn't be matched in private schools.

Parents must understand that they may actually be helping the development of their children when they work together, as a team, to find appropriate compromises relative to expenditures on their children. Helping, and not spoiling, the children will be the result of this effort. Remember that although we didn't have nearly as many of these "advantages" and "open doors" available when growing up, we made it through life without these "advantages". Keep in mind that opening doors for your children should not mean closing doors for yourself. Remember there is no shame in limiting their activities to those that you can afford.

We try to give our spouse everything as well—fancy restaurants, nice vacations, luxury cars, designer clothes, tickets to a show or concert, etc. While we want to make our spouse happy, we need to consider whether, he/she is really much happier as a result of these expenditures. Both you and your spouse should be pleased to see funds going into investments every month instead of having nothing left or bills you can't pay at the end of the month. But this doesn't necessarily mean you need to feel deprived. There can be a feeling of satisfaction in going out for an evening visiting friends, receiving a thoughtful but inexpensive birthday gift, or taking a driving vacation instead of a lavish cruise (save the lavish cruise for the retirement years). Watching the nest egg grow will be a source of satisfaction that will last much longer than the memories of the concert or play.

Buying Gifts—Anniversaries and birthdays can put a big hole in your pocketbook if you're not careful. Buying an expensive piece of jewelry every year for your wife can be a costly proposition. Don't forget there are birthdays, anniversaries, and Valentine's Day to say nothing about some additional Hallmark holidays still being invented. While it's important to buy a thoughtful gift for your spouse, you don't need to break the bank doing it.

A piece of jewelry should be something you buy as a special gift, rather than an expected gift many times a year. Be creative. Your spouse will appreciate it more. How about giving flowers. It takes thoughtfulness, more than money, to select an appropriate gift. Find out if there is something in particular that your spouse would like as a gift by observing your spouse and if that fails, come right out and ask. It's better not to waste your money by purchasing something he/she doesn't want.

For example, my wife loves to read. So I try to figure out what book she would like for her birthday and get her that along with a little inexpensive surprise gift. Flowers are always appreciated and need not cost much more than $25. Occasionally, purchase tickets to a ballet, opera, concert, or whatever your spouse really would enjoy, as a special gift. It may cost a couple of hundred dollars, but it is something you should do once in a while. It's also nice to go out to an upscale restaurant for birthdays and anniversaries. Limiting it to once or twice a year make the occasions special. Once every few years, buy a nice piece of jewelry or arrange for a vacation as an anniversary gift for both of you.

6.2 Transportation

Driving has become an adventure in spending. However it is necessary to get to and from work as well as participate in a host of family and personal activities. We can hardly see ourselves surviving with just public transportation or even actually walking or bicycling to work even if work is nearby. So, we must recognize the need for a car as a modern necessity. The most important thing to consider is whether you are driving the right car and whether you are using it wisely.

The New Car—Some people will say that there is nothing like the smell of a new car. Driving a new car is always exhilarating. There are those who feel it even compares favorably to sex. New cars look great and give one an emotional lift. But should you purchase the best car that the dealer will finance? Big, big mistake! We somehow forget that for most of us a car should be nothing more than a means of transportation. The additional cost and monthly premiums we pay for the benefit of driving an upscale brand new car, which remains new for only a few weeks, is hardly justified.

Spending $30,000 (or $40,000) on a new car when a new $20,000 car will work for you is a waste of $10,000 (or $20,000) that you could put away for your retirement and invest to grow until you're ready to retire. You can also put away the higher monthly car loan interest charges. Never purchase a larger (and more expensive) car than you need since other related costs including gasoline, repairs, tires, financing, etc. all tend to be significantly higher for the larger car. The smaller car would likely have a longer life as well. Do you realize that wasting $10,000 on the purchase of a car every 5 years could have resulted in an increased nest egg of $150,000 (invested properly) after 25-years? What, you're actually a two-car family. You're probably approaching $250,000 now.

The Used Car—True, your car needs to be reliable, since you need to get to work on time and it's no fun waiting for a tow truck on the side of the road. Consider buying a fairly new, reliable, used foreign car with exceptional gas mileage. The cost savings from purchasing cars used will add even more to that $250,000 savings discussed above. And you will still have reliable transportation. Not a bad deal.

It takes a lot of patience to locate a suitable used car. Purchasing from a stranger through newspaper ads can seem like a crapshoot. Purchasing from a used car lot is only slightly more reliable. However, if it's a relatively new (2-3 years old) used car, it may come with the manufacturers warrantee still in effect. For older cars, consider purchasing through a commercial new and used car dealer who guarantees the car for 30-90 days. Check with your coworkers and keep an eye out for a good buy on a quality used car.

Public Transportation and Carpooling—Try to reduce your commuting cost if possible. Taking public transportation is a fuel-saving and less expensive way to get to work. Using the train or bus will not only reduce the wear and tear on your car but on your nerves as well. Reading the newspaper and snoozing on a commuter train will get you to work far more refreshed than 45 minutes of white knuckle driving in heavy traffic.

Another option is to join or form a carpool. This would split the cost of driving by the number of fellow travelers. Don't forget the savings in tolls and the additional enhancement of good company to make the trip more pleasant. Car-pooling is frequently inconvenient. However you should recognize the potential savings. If you do the math, you will find that driving a car costs about 50 cents/mile on average. Figure out what you would save and decide if carpooling is the right option for you.

Signing your children up for a number of activities often results in making many, many extra car trips in the course of a week. Therefore you should keep this in mind when you determine if you should enroll your children in so many activities. Provide them with a list of activities and ask them to select their favorite two or three. Then, once you meet some of the parents, try carpooling to these activities and save on mileage and perhaps make a new friend or two. The best idea might be to just stay home and give the children some good old attention that they thrive on. Pull out one of the board games stashed away in the closet and gathering dust or just do some arts-and-crafts together.

Running Errands—We can, and usually do, spend the majority of the weekend running errands. Yet we seldom stop to figure out the cost of driving on all of these errands. With the cost of gasoline flying out of sight, we need to try to consolidate these errands. Make a list of what you need to do and then do them in an organized manner to minimize the mileage driven. Going to a number of different stores to save $2 does not make sense if you are spending more on transportation than you're saving. If you drive an extra 3 miles each way (for a total of 6 miles) it costs you about $3 plus your time. The mileage on these errands adds up in a hurry.

6.3 Entertainment

Today's American spends more money on entertainment than ever before. We feel we are entitled to get maximum enjoyment out of life and don't mind digging into our wallets (or swiping our credit cards) to pay for this fun. Some of our favorite activities include concerts, ballgames, golf outings, family vacations, movies, plays, etc. All of these can add up in a hurry. We often forget that there are other forms of entertainment that can be enjoyed without burning a hole in one's wallet.

Let's look at ways to reduce entertainment costs without eliminating the fun.

An Outing for the Whole Family—Take the entire family of four out for dinner and a movie and you've probably spent well over $100. Take them out to an NBA basketball game or to the theater and you've likely spent over $300 including dinner. Do this once a month and you've spent $4,000 for the year. Ouch!!! Save half this amount every year, for 25 years, and you could increase your nest egg by over $150,000. Does this mean that you stay at home every weekend and never go out? Definitely not! You'll just need to look for more cost effective outings. Consider the following:

- Go to the park and play baseball, go roller skating, or bike riding as a family and then enjoy a picnic or a pizza afterwards
- Spend a day at the beach and bring along a picnic lunch basket
- Eat at home and attend a free or inexpensive local concert in the evening
- Visit the zoo or the arboretum
- Play miniature golf and then rent a movie and bring in a pizza for dinner
- Visit with relatives and help (or watch) the cousins, aunts and uncles play football in the backyard
- Let's not forget visiting the grandparents. Nothing will put a sparkle in their eye and a spring in their step like a visit from their little angels. It's even uplifting for the kids too
- Take walks in the park or on the beach

Going to the Movies—Many families go to the movies just to have something to do. Let's look at what this costs: Maybe $30 for a family of four just to get into the theater. Another $ 20 will likely be spent for beverages and snacks. Don't forget the cost of gasoline and use of your car to get there. By the time you're finished you've spent more than $50 for a movie that is probably no better than one you could have rented to watch at home for $4. Plus you could enjoy your own popcorn from the microwave. This would have saved you $40 and you could take off your shoes and be much more comfortable as well.

Do this once a month and you've saved close to $500 for the year. Did you have a really great time for your money—probably not? Limit the nights out at the movies to special occasion, perhaps once every couple of months or whenever there is a real special new movie playing and everyone will appreciate it more.

Enjoy the Public Library—One of the problems in this country is that nobody seems to read any more. We want instant gratification by seeing the whole story in an hour or two on the big screen. We are missing out on the true beauty and emotions of the story and the opportunity to experience the feelings that a book affords.

Don't pay $30 for the book. Go to the public library and take out the book for free. Put the book on reserve, wait a few weeks, and you'll appreciate the book even more when your e-mail announces that the book is waiting for you. It's almost like receiving a gift. Also think about going to used-book sales at the library or elsewhere and purchasing a novel in reasonably good condition for $3.

You can save money by renting movies from the library. Most libraries charge a nominal fee (perhaps $1 per movie) while others are sometimes free. The latest movies may require a waiting list of a few weeks. So what! You'll enjoy the movie just the same and save many dollars along the way. Once your e-mail announces that the movie is waiting for you, you can turn the "gift" into a nice family night at home.

Children can go through many movies in the course of a week, at a $4 rental, it adds up fast. So take that short trip to the library and grab a movie or two off the shelf and add a bag of microwaveable popcorn, then rain-or-shine, their weekend is set.

There are often events and book readings at libraries that may peak your interest. Consider author book signings, movie-showings, book discussion groups, and mini-courses that you or your spouse might enjoy. Also, your children can find activities at the library that they'll enjoy. It is always a good idea to get your children away from the TV and computer for the afternoon while they are still in their formative stages and willing to consider new ideas. As a parent, you know that this is no small accomplishment.

Museums—Museums and galleries are found in most areas. There's typically something there that will grab your fancy. Consider buying a family membership as an inducement to participate in cultural activities. Activities like exhibits, lectures, movie-showings, discussions, and sometimes even classes makes museum membership a bargain. Taking children to museums is another good way of giving them a cultural education that they wouldn't get otherwise from television or text messaging back and forth with their friends.

Gambling—Many of us have an itch we like to scratch from time to time known as gambling. Between horseracing, lotteries, riverboat casinos and Indian casinos it's hard to avoid the temptation. We even like to go to Las Vegas on vacation where there is little to do but gamble all day and night. It is impossible not to notice just how glamorous the new, modern casinos are. Did you ever wonder where the money came from to build these casinos? It comes from gamblers like you.

The casinos refer to the games and slot machines you play as "gambling". That is what they want you to believe. The casinos can estimate how much money they will make on a daily basis. Does this sound like they are "gambling"? If they're not gambling on their daily returns, it goes to say that you cannot be gambling either and will eventually lose. The odds are stacked against you. You might win once in awhile but if you play long enough, you will lose, since the games and slot machines are designed accordingly. Are you "gambling" or paying for entertainment? It's alright to go to Atlantic City or Las Vegas or any other casino as long as you recognize that your are not gambling, but paying for entertainment. Who knows, you might win on occasion. But not in the long run. Don't take more money with you than the value, to you, of the entertainment for the day or evening.

The other forms of "gambling" such as horse racing, dog racing, jai alai, and certain Internet games are all designed to make it difficult for you to win over the long run. And don't forget the "good old" lottery tickets. These are just taxes that you go out of your way to pay. It is often referred to as a "tax on the poor". The lottery can wreak havoc on an individual's finances, especially those in lower-income groups. So just don't do it.

Internet Access and Cable Costs—The cable companies love you. They can't do enough for you. They now bundle all sorts of wonderful entertainment packages and you only need to pay them once a month. For close to $100 per month you can have 160 cable TV channels, DSL or cable Internet service, as well as unlimited telephone service. For another $60 you can supplement your phone bill with a great cell phone package with a "free" phone that takes pictures and can connect to the Internet as well. Do the math and you'll find that this adds up to a total of roughly $2,000 per year.

Compare this to the "old days", which was actually only 15 years ago. Cable service was not always available and there were only nine television stations to watch. But it was free. Telephone service cost roughly $30 per month and there was no cell phone usage. There also was no wide spread Internet use. Is it any wonder that life is more expensive today? Now what to do?

Those who need to be especially thrifty could avoid cable TV and cell phone use entirely. This would leave them with just telephone and DSL computer service. They would save 70% of the annual $2,000 cost. Alternatively, they could purchase the cheapest cable service available and it will only give you 50 channels to "surf until you drop". Then take the least expensive DSL service available along with an inexpensive telephone package coupled with the least expensive cell phone package. Creating your own plan like this will cut your costs nearly in half and you would have more technology then you ever had or even know what to do with.

Computer Envy—There are ways to use your computer to save money. Start sending electronic birthday and anniversary cards (except maybe for that special someone). People enjoy them far more and they can save you a bunch of money. The $20 annual cost to sign up with one of the electronic greeting card companies for the year is well worth the cost. With the price of greeting cards going out of sight, you can easily save over $100 for the year.

I find that people really enjoy the funny, animated cards. My grandchildren, who are just becoming comfortable with computers, get a real kick out of receiving a few animated cards for their birthdays. I also inundate my wife with a number of electronic cards on her birthday and on our anniversary. It almost makes up for us not being able to spend the entire day together. In the evening I give her a store bought Hallmark card along with a thoughtful (and usually somewhat inexpensive) gift.

Sending e-mail to friends and relatives is a great, inexpensive way, to stay in touch. You can keep people informed of the latest family occurrences and keep them all up to date if someone is ill. It certainly beats trying to call 15 people to tell them how the surgery went. In addition, paying your bills over the internet can save you time and the cost of postage as well as allowing you to earn interest on your money until the day the payment is actually due.

Computers have become such a large part of our lives that it is rare to find a computer at home or at work in the shut down mode. There are so many worthwhile things that you can do on the computer, such as keeping track of your investments and expenses, typing letters and reports, figuring out work-related projects, and sometimes just browsing the internet for information or checking for the best price on an item you need to purchase can be helpful but it can also become addictive, leading to your spending much more than you planned. Frequently an Internet purchase comes with free shipping which is great for providing gifts on time to say nothing about saving you the time and cost of going shopping.

Be careful you don't spend too much time browsing for different products or you may be enticed into purchasing things you don't really need. Don't be fooled by all the e-mails that you'll get about saving money by purchasing things you can do without. Resist those "work from home" ads that take advantage of those who need extra spending money. After all who doesn't? The jobs sound great and all you need to do is send them $19.95 for a "kit" of some kind. Do you realize that they receive tens of thousands of responses to their e-mail? That adds up to millions of dollars they receive. They then send out "kits" that are nearly worthless and there are very few real jobs available.

Be especially careful of gambling sites. Gambling is an ugly, expensive, habit that will seem enticing while you're sitting at the computer in your slippers. These sites get to be very addictive.

6.4 Food and Drugs

Restaurants—Two people having a decent meal with all the trimmings in a good restaurant can easily pay over $100 for the dinner. It seems so easy to take out your credit card and pay the check for $100 (or more) for a dinner for two. Do this just once a week and you have an additional $400 added to your credit card bill. Then the credit card bill comes in and is typically paid without scrutinizing each item too carefully, allowing these restaurant charges to get lost amid all the necessary items like groceries and gasoline expenditures included in the bill. You may not even notice the cost of that dinner.

Dining out is always an enjoyable experience. However, if done too often, it can get to be an expense that most people can't afford. This author doesn't suggest you stop going to restaurants but just be aware of how to avoid eating yourself out of house and home (and retirement). This does not mean that you always cook at home or that you eat at fast food restaurants where the quality of the food is poor. But you need to be aware of how restaurant costs add up and how to keep them under control.

Limiting the class of restaurant you visit along with controlling overly expensive items on the menu such as alcoholic beverages and fancy desserts can reduce your restaurant bill substantially.

Eating out in a family restaurant or diner is far more affordable than upscale restaurants. The difference in cost between the two types of restaurants can save a couple over $50 for dinner each time they eat out. Saving $70 per week by judiciously choosing restaurants and avoiding excessively expensive items, results in saving $3500 per year. This can grow to nearly a quarter of a million dollars over a 25-year period. The potential savings is even greater when you consider taking the whole family for dinner and the fact that most couples eat out more than once a week. So go ahead and enjoy dining out but control your costs and you can literally have your cake and eat it too.

There are other ways to control your restaurant costs. Many local restaurants, as well as some restaurant chains, provide buy-one-get one free coupons that can save you quite a lot if you control what you order. But be careful. The restaurants are willing to give away an entrée in the hope that you will order alcoholic beverages and dessert, which result in huge profits for them. But you can save many dollars at a sitting just by vigilantly clipping meal coupons. Look for mailings and check the local newspapers for these coupons. Some restaurants even have printable coupons on their web sites. So, next time you order a pizza, check for coupons.

Lunch Money and Snacks—Many workers believe it's impossible to get through a day without leaving the office to go out for lunch. Be careful not to get caught up in this since it is a costly luxury. Restaurant lunches can easily add $25 per week to the cost of bringing your own lunch from home. This adds up to more than $1,000 per year. This sum could grow to close to $75,000 over a 25-year period. Note that the potential savings can go much higher if you occasionally order alcoholic beverages with your lunch "just to relax". Were those lunches really that good?

There is no reason not to occasionally enjoy lunches with your co-workers as long as you don't make a habit of it. Bring your own bag lunch to work most of the week and you will find yourself not only with more money in your pocket but less fat on your waste and lower cholesterol in your blood. Besides you will enjoy the lunch out as an occasional treat.

Does it make sense to save that lunch money and then buy a five-dollar cup of coffee at one of the popular upscale coffee chains or stop for a fast food breakfast? Make the time to eat a solid breakfast at home and have a home-brewed cup of coffee before leaving for work. That cup of coffee, made by the coffee maker that you spent twenty dollars on ten years ago, is probably good enough. Coffee at work is normally free (or some modest cost like 25 cents a cup). It may not taste the greatest, but stick with it. It sure beats running across the street to spend five-dollars on a large frothy cup. The latte or some other foamy rich drink is not worth what they charge. Along these same lines, fight the urge to purchase an overpriced, super-duper high cholesterol muffin to go with it. It's striking to think how much money you're depriving your retirement of by these daily out-of-pocket luxuries. It could pay for quite a few overseas vacations for two in your retirement years.

Groceries—An average American family of four spends well in excess of $10,000 a year on groceries. Even if you cut only 10% from that, you'll save $1,000 a year. That's a sizeable annual savings that will add up over the years. If you want to save even more, you could use coupons, purchase store brands, and cut down on convenience foods. It really is not that difficult to accumulate and utilize coupons and ends up in a savings of at least another 5-10% of your grocery budget.

A great way to cut down your grocery bill is to shop at more than one grocery store to ensure that you purchase your groceries as inexpensively as reasonable. However don't ignore the cost of gasoline and car expenses when deciding how many stores to frequent. You will notice that grocery stores all run sales to attract customers and then make up for their losses on other items. The best approach is to buy what's on sale along with what you need for the coming week. Then stock your pantry and freezer with discounted items. But don't purchase groceries you typically don't use just because they are on sale. Supermarket sales run in cycles, with different types of products going on sale each week. Items on the front page of the weekly supermarket circular frequently offer the best deals. Keep track of the prices on food you repeatedly buy so you'll know when an item truly is on sale. You will sacrifice nothing in quality or selection while saving money by doing this correctly.

Brand Names—Some people always purchase brand names at the supermarket and drug store because they think they're superior. This is sometimes true, but many brand names are not worth the extra cost. The store brand is often just as good as name brands that cost much more. Commodity items such as sugar, salt, flour, etc are actually identical and buying store brands can save you up to 50%. Try store brands and see if you can tell the difference. Then determine for yourself whether the difference in quality, if any, is worth the savings.

The chain store brand of some over-the-counter drug products can also save you quite a lot of money. For example the store brand mouthwash might cost 30-50% less than the brand name item so check the list of active ingredients and see if you can tell them apart. Try the chain store brand and decide for yourself if the item meets your needs.

Bottled water is better for your health than sweetened soft drinks. But even the store brand is a waste of money to say nothing of the brands with those exotic sounding French names. Analysis of bottled water has found it no more "special" than good old American filtered tap water. If you have a refrigerator with a built-in water dispenser with a carbon canister, you're in business. Make a habit of putting a pitcher of filtered water with ice on the table for all meals. It's a great routine to get your children into at home and in restaurants.

Medications—Generic drugs are drugs whose patents have expired and are then marketed under their formulation by any pharmaceutical company who chooses to produce them. Once the patent runs out and competition is created, the price of the drug drops very significantly (frequently more than 50%). The active ingredients in generic drugs are mostly similar to those in name-brand drugs and just as effective, although they may have different quantities of fillers added.

The insurance companies recognize the similarity and penalize your co-payment charge very significantly if you don't substitute an available generic drug. Doctors generally write prescriptions for the medication they typically prescribe. They do not stop to think that with health insurance there can be major cost differences between the prescribed medication and an equally effective generic drug. Few patients would think to ask the doctor whether or not the prescription is for a generic medication. They do not question the doctor and believe this is the only medication that will work. There is no harm in asking the question—Is this generic? If it is not, ask if there is a generic alternative that the doctor feels comfortable prescribing. Often, the doctor only needs to check the box in his prescription letting the pharmacist know whether a generic version of the drug can be substituted. Your savings can easily be $100 for some prescriptions and much more if you require multiple renewals. Depending on how many times your family visits the doctor, the annual savings can be over $1,000.

Don't overlook store brand over-the-counter medications like antihistamines, cold pills, cough medicine, bandages, tape, aspirin, ibuprofen, etc. The store brand is generally 25-35% less expensive but some can save you even more. For example generic aspirin at a chain drug store may be priced at roughly $1 per bottle of 100 tablets while the well known name brand can cost over $3 per bottle for the same pills. So be aware of what you purchase at the pharmacy.

6.5 Let's Get Physical

Financial and physical well-being—Your physical well-being can be linked to your financial health if you look to avoid expenses by making it a practice to do the household chores yourself. It is also a good idea to teach your children about responsibility by having them earn their allowances by doing some of the chores and errands. This approach will save you money and will be a good lesson for your children.

If you are reasonably healthy, you should not have to pay (except perhaps to your own kids) for lawn mowing, snow shoveling, house cleaning, car washing, etc. Doing these things for yourself will burn calories, help keep you fit, and also keep those precious dollars in your pocket. Even consider walking (or biking) on errands to a local store.

Joining a health club—Many people need encouragement to keep themselves fit so they join health clubs in the hope that the group effect will keep them interested. Health clubs typically have the latest equipment and provide professional advice. But are these costs justified? You might consider joining the local Y, and living with their 5 year-old exercise equipment. You can save even more by just exercising on your own. All you will need is an inexpensive set of weights, a pair of running shoes, and a bike (or stationary bike). A word of caution is to not spend too much on the equipment (except for the running shoes) since an inexpensive or second hand bike will give you more exercise than a brand new streamlined model and old weights work as well as new weights. Buy second hand since there is a good chance that they'll all end up in the closet or basement gathering dust. Never buy new exercise clothing. Old ratty looking clothes are meant for sweat.

The advantage of exercising on your own is that you'll have the equipment at hand so you can take advantage of using it any time, even if your spouse is out and you need to watch the children. Use the stationary bike and keep an eye on your children or leave them doing homework while you get (stay) fit at home. Plus you'll be setting a good example for them.

Besides saving the monthly health club cost (typically more than $50), not to mention the designer workout clothes, you will also save travel time and cost to the health club. Assuming you drive 15 minutes each way and allow another few minutes to change clothes, you will cut your total time spent on a 45 minute workout by close to 50%. This may make your workouts more feasible.

They're Hazardous to Your Health—Americans have, to a great extent, stopped smoking. Education and the Surgeon General's remarks coupled with huge cigarette taxes have finally gotten most people to drop this horrible habit.

Sure, a pack of smokes isn't cheap (especially in areas like New York City, where they cost about $7) but don't forget to add the impact that a lifelong smoking habit would have on your life expectancy, insurance premiums, medical care, and lost earnings due to illness.

The cost of cigarettes, alone, could easily result in a loss of over $100,000 to your retirement nest egg. That's a lot of money going up in smoke. But the heavy smoker doesn't need to worry about it since he likely will not have too many retirement years anyway. It's interesting to note that the additional life expectancy of nonsmokers results in their receiving an extra $5,000 in Social Security payments that smokers miss out on due to their shorter life.

Obesity—This is another recent challenge facing middle-aged people. Without getting into definitions here, just recognize that the number of people morbidly obese is phenomenal. Close to 50% of future retirees will be either fat or obese. Why does this happen? There are a number of reasons including eating fast foods, restaurant meals, and desserts in combination with inadequate exercise. What has become especially frightening is the level of obesity in our children. We need to serve as a better example for them.

Everyone needs to eat properly. Probably the worst eating habit is snacking. Shoppers can help the chronic snacker in their household by having only healthy snacks in the house. Put apples, raisins, and whole grain items on your shopping list instead of cookies, ice cream, potato chips, fruit loops, and white bread. Then stick with the list, no matter how tempting that cookie aisle may be. Unhealthy snack foods are overpriced as well. So save money and save your family's health at the same time.

6.6 Miscellaneous Consumer Expenses

Clothing—Employees almost always spend too much money on clothing for work. Is there some clothing pageant that is going on at the office that requires a man to own a number of $300 suits, two $200 sport jackets, ten different button-down shirts, five expensive sweaters, three pairs of casual pants (for dress-down days) and five pairs of dress shoes? At least a man's wardrobe for home is typically filled with inexpensive jeans, tees, sweats, and a few pairs of footwear.

Women, not to be outdone in the workplace, must have multiple outfits (or business suits), two weeks worth of skirts, blouses, and dress slacks. In addition they might collect 10 to 20 pairs of shoes. At home, clothing needs will likely include sun-dresses, short skirts, sweatshirts, sweat pants, shorts, tees, and designer exercise suits, in addition to many, many pairs of footwear. The shorts, sweats and tees are usually (but not always) inexpensive but the footwear can cost an arm and a leg if you're not careful. Typical sports footwear goes for $100 per pair and most have a pair for jogging, another for tennis, and another just to knock around on the weekend.

You can dress appropriately for work while being rational about what you spend. It's okay to avoid the upscale stores generally found at the local mall and go to chain stores like J.C. Penney's, Kohl's or Target. Sometimes even Wal-Mart and K-Mart will suit your needs and save you even more money. Remember nobody is going to know where you purchased your clothes. It's not like you're going to have to look the other way or hide if you see a fellow employee trying on clothes in the fitting area of Target. You're not in high school anymore. You can save considerable amounts by purchasing clothing at the end of the season when the stores mark down prices by as much as 75%. There is no reason to purchase sweats and exercise wear from a sporting goods store when you can shop at a local K-Mart or Wal-Mart. Exercise footwear, on the other hand, should be purchased in a sporting goods store. But take advantage of end of the season sales and discontinued styles. You can easily save 40% or more.

Buying clothes for your children for school can be a major annual expense. You should look for opportunities to hand down clothes from older children. Don't be afraid to discuss this openly with your friends and relatives as well. You can all save a bunch of money by trading off clothing as your kids outgrow their clothes. Don't fall into the trap of purchasing designer clothes for your children. They don't wear any better and cost twice as much. Buy the cheap imitations and you will have serviceable products just the same. Your kids are going to outgrow, or rip, the clothes much sooner than wear them out anyway.

Insurance—Most people don't understand insurance so they don't ask appropriate questions and tend to purchase what the agent planned to sell. Remember that the main purpose of insurance is to protect against catastrophic loss, not all the little things. So by keeping your deductibles high, you will come out ahead in the long run by paying lower premiums and avoiding frivolous claims.

Life insurance is only appropriate for people who have someone else truly relying on their income. Insurance agents will take advantage of people's ignorance on this subject and tell you that you need coverage for stay-at-home spouses to compensate for the child-care and other domestic duties of the at-home spouse. This is something you should weigh carefully before taking the plunge. Maybe this is one risk you should take. Children don't need life insurance as a means to save money. They have plenty of time to start saving for themselves. Young childless couples have time to buy insurance when a family is dependant on the breadwinner. Retirees, and people in the 50s, will pay a small fortune for life insurance. Once you're retired, you shouldn't need life insurance since by then your dependents should be self-sufficient.

Whole life (cash value) life insurance consists of both protection and savings. Although whole life policies build up cash value, there are certainly better ways to put your money to work either through investing or paying off those pesky credit card debts. Most families need the protection that life insurance offers. Term life insurance provides only the protection component and is significantly less expensive than the whole life plan since there is no savings portion of the policy. Buying term insurance will allow you to purchase much more protection and still have money left over. You should evaluate converting your cash-value policy to a term plan. Check carefully with an insurance specialist before canceling any policy so that you understand the ramifications of this change.

It also makes sense to look for savings in your auto insurance. Consider raising your deductibles, as this will reduce your premiums. Raise your deductibles to a level that will pinch you but not break you in the event of a claim. Chances are good that you'll save money in the long run and you'll be less likely to have to file a claim for small repairs. Filing damage claims can increase your premiums, and your insurer may even drop your coverage. Too many people carry costly collision insurance on an old car with a very low book value. They take out collision coverage when the car is new and don't reevaluate the plan as the car ages. So an annual review of your coverage with your agent can be very worthwhile.

Always shop around for auto, home, and life insurance. Prices vary widely. An average American family of four spends over $3,000 on insurance annually.

Even if you save only 10% of that, it's well worth your while. If you do decide to switch packages, make sure that the new company is legitimate by checking with your state insurance department.

6.7 Your Personal Savings Scorecard

The pages above have provided some ideas on how you might reduce your monthly and annual expenses. Although many of these concepts may not be ideal for you, it's likely that you will find a number that do apply. Let's look at the potential impact of adopting just a few of these ideas. The table below is a "grab bag" of potential items intended to illustrate the magnitude of the total savings that most people can avail themselves of.

Item	Monthly Savings	Annual Savings
Eliminating professional lawn care including mowing, fertilizing, trimming	100	600
Car washing yourself	25	300
Rent movies from library	15	180
Don't purchase coffee and donuts	100	1200
Eliminate health club cost	50	600
Take lunch to work	100	1200
Own used car instead of new car (annualized)	150	1800
Reduce car usage	15	180
Less costly family outings	50	600
Purchase super market and store brands	50	600
Eat at family restaurants instead of upscale restaurants	100	1200
Shop for clothing in chain stores	50	600
TOTAL	$ 805	$9,060

It's hard to believe that just a hand full of the ideas presented above could easily result in saving around $10,000 per year. But pennies add up in a hurry. Keep in mind that many of these "sacrifices" are really just bad habits that need to be corrected anyway. In reality you will have sacrificed very little of true value and stand to gain much over the years.

You should utilize these savings to first eliminate your debts and then begin investing the saved money for your later years. Saving $10,000 per year for 25 years will result in an additional $600,000 in your nest egg by the time you're ready to retire. Add these funds with the other funds you put away in your IRAs and 401(k) plans and you're on your way. Now is the time to get started.

This chapter focused on saving money so that you can first pay down your debts and then have money available to build for your future. The next Chapters will focus on how to increase the value of this saved money.

Chapter 7

Saving for Your Future

Everybody wants to know how much money he or she will need to save in order to be prepared for retirement. This is not an easy question to answer. It depends on a number of factors including:

- How much income will come from your pensions and Social Security?
- How well do you want to live?
- How much debt do you have?
- How long will you live?
- How healthy will you be?
- What unexpected expenses will you have?
- How will your investments fare?
- How much inflation will there be?

Of the above factors, only the first three items are quantifiable. Therefore, unless you are rolling in dough, you can only save as much as possible and hope that the other variables are within reason.

Most people think in terms of round numbers like $500,000, $1,000,000, and $2,000,000. What will you need? Good question. Your exact needs will depend on the above factors, most of which are out of your control. But suffice it to say that most people don't need anywhere near $1,000,000 to have a long enjoyable retirement. Let's explore some of the factors that will impact whether you can reach your personal retirement goals.

7.1 The Miracle of Compounding

Saving and investing are the cornerstones of paying for your financial future. A large, lump-sum investment is great if you inherit money or are wealthy to begin with. If not, a good savings plan comprised of frequent contributions is a great substitute for starting out rich. The secret to financial success is to utilize the "miracle of compounding" to grow your wealth by taking advantage of the time value of money. Compounding is the royal road to riches and fortunately anybody can ride that road. Let's explore what compounding means.

If you ask workers how much money they would have if they had $10,000 in an account earning 10% for two years, the results are surprising. The majority of people would say the account would be worth $12,000 after two years. Some people would not even be able to answer the question at all. But few would recognize that the real value of the account would be $12,100 due to the interest earned in the second year on the interest from the first year. This is compound interest and the extra $100 in the example builds up to quite a lot over 25 or 30 years.

The following Table shows how investing $10,000 at the end of each year will grow over time utilizing a historically conservative 6% return on an after-tax basis. This can be compared to placing the $10,000 in a tax deferred plan growing at 8%. The amount of accumulated wealth that this 2% difference can make over 30 years is staggering.

$10,000 per Year Compound Interest Table

	Total Invested at $10,000 per year	Accumulated Amount @ 8% (tax deferred)	Accumulated Amount @ 6% (after taxes)
	$ 50,000	$ 58,666	$ 56,371
10	$ 100,000	$ 144,866	$ 131,808
20	$ 200,000	$ 457,620	$ 367,858
25	$ 250,000	$ 731,059	$ 548,645
30	$ 300,000	$ 1,132,832	$ 790,582

The numbers in the above table illustrate the magic of compound interest. Investing $10,000 per year for 30 years totals $ 300,000. If you invest those funds in a tax deferred account growing at 8% for 30 years and you'll have roughly $1,100,000. This is almost a 4-fold increase in value. Even the after-tax 6% return will grow to much more than double the $300,000 that you saved and invested.

What do you need to do to take advantage of compounding?

- Time to allow the power of compounding to work for you. Start today, compounding only works over time.
- Perseverance to keep you from straying from the savings path.

So how do you get started? Take advantage of company-sponsored savings plans like 401(k) plans and change your behavior to reduce your spending enough to bring your annual savings to at least $10,000. The illustrations in Chapter 6 show that it's really not that difficult to reduce your expenses by $10,000 per year. If you then invest effectively, you will have quite a nest egg. Combine these funds with Social Security and you have reached the point that you dreamed about. Even without a pension, one can live quite well in retirement.

What if you can't put away $10,000 yearly? Should you just shrug and go on living "fat, dumb, and happy"? **No**!!! You can still make a sizeable impact on your retirement nest egg with whatever you can save. The following Table shows future values of an account with more modest savings expressed as monthly contributions. The chart is based on starting with only $1,000 and an investment growth rate of 8% a year. You will note that the accumulated amounts in this chart are quite substantial. This will leave you with a significant amount of money upon retiring, perhaps enough depending on how the unknown factors described at the beginning of this chapter develop.

8% Growth Rate at Different Monthly Investment Amounts

Years of Savings:	Future Value of Account Based on These Monthly Contributions:			
	$ 0/month	$ 100/month	$ 250/month	$ 500/month
1	$ 1,000	$ 2,200	$ 4,000	$ 7,000
5	$ 1,360	$ 8,400	$ 19,000	$ 3,700
10	$ 2,000	$ 19,400	$ 45,500	$ 89,000
30	$ 9,300	$ 145,000	$ 349,000	$ 689,000

As the table indicates, putting aside only $250 per month for 30 years could result in nearly $350,000 upon reaching retirement. If you add this to your Social Security you have a fighting chance. Now, if you also have a 401(k) plan you're in pretty good shape.

7.2 The Value of Starting Early

To take maximum advantage of compound returns you need to start early. Unfortunately, none of us have yet figured out how to turn back the clock to those earlier years when we should have acted more wisely. Too many people procrastinate, delaying to begin saving and investing. They don't realize just how much a little good old deprivation today can greatly reduce sorrow tomorrow.

To illustrate the value of starting early we will compare a person who starts an IRA at the age of 25 (called "Early Starter") with a person, the same age, who waits 10 years to start (called "Late Bloomer"). In the following example, we will have "Early Starter" invest $2,000 each year (at 8% after tax return) for 10 years and then stop. Then "Late Bloomer" will start investing $2,000 every year starting at the age of 35 while "Early Starter" stops saving, going into financial hibernation. It would be foolish for the "Early Starter" to stop saving but we are trying to illustrate a point.

The results for both individuals are compared in the table below.

	Early Starter Amount Saved	*Early Starter* Value of Savings	*Late Bloomer* Amount Saved	*Late Bloomer* Value of Savings
@ 35 Years of Age	$ 20,000	$ 29,000	$ 0	$ 0
@ 65 Years of Age	$ 20,000	$ 290,000	$ 60,000	$ 226,000

The numbers are hard to believe but Late Bloomer never could catch up. Even after 30 years. "Early Starter" would have invested only $20,000 ($2,000 for each of 10 years), but had $290,000 at age 65. Meanwhile, "Late Bloomer" would have invested a total of $60,000 ($2,000 for each of 30 years). Remarkably, he would have less of a nest egg, only $226,000 at age 65. In this way, "Late Bloomer" got less for more. Truly unbelievable isn't it?

The "Early Starter", who made his/her contributions earlier and who made only ten contributions, ends up with **MORE** money than "Late Bloomer", who made 30 contributions but at a **LATER TIME**. The difference is that the early starter has ten more early years of compounding which more than doubled his money and then the magic of compounding just took over.

There is no substitute for starting early and allowing the "magic of compounding" to get you to your goal. The inescapable lesson here is to **START TODAY** since you can't turn back the clock.

7.3 The Ravages of Inflation

What is inflation? It is a general price rise in goods and services that decreases the purchasing power of your dollar. $1,000,000 may seem like a small fortune today. But in 40 years it may only be able to buy what $200,000 can buy today. Inflation works against you, partially negating the magic of compounding to reduce the true value of your nest egg.

Nobody is quite sure what inflation will do to the purchasing power of the dollar over the next 30 or 40 years. But you can be sure that it'll take much more money to buy the same goods and services in the future. Let's take a look at what inflation did to the average price of some common items over the last 40 years.

Item	Cost in 1968	Cost in 2006	% Increase
Average Single Family Home (according to the Nat'l Board of Realtors)	$ 20,100	$ 221,900	1000
Movie Theater Admission (per Nat'l Assoc of Theater Owners)	$ 1.31	$ 6.55	400
Annual College Costs including room and board at a 4 year in-state Public University (per Nat'l Center for Education Statistics)	$ 1,245	$ 12,796	930
Loaf of Bread (per Bureau of Labor Statistics)	$ .25	$ 1.08	330
Gallon of Gasoline (per Energy Information Administration)	$ 34	$ 2.58	660

As the table above indicates common goods that you will still be purchasing in retirement like food, gasoline, and movie tickets have gone up anywhere from 3 times to 7 times in price over the last 40 years. Other large ticket items like college costs and single-family homes have gone up even more. But you will not be paying for these items in retirement.

7.4 Pay Yourself First

You should contribute to your savings first, before you have a chance to spend the money on something else. After all we all can find unlimited ways to spend our money. But make sure you pay yourself in the following ways:

- Through tax deferred 401(k) plans through your employer (if available). Your employer will automatically deduct your contributions before you get your hands on the remainder.
- Through a personal IRA account. You will need to make the contribution yourself.
- Through personal savings and investing. You will again need to make the payments yourself.

The money you save by reducing your spending by following the blueprint presented in previous chapters will allow you to take advantage of these cornerstones of saving. Hopefully you will take advantage of all three factors mentioned above.

The first priority is to maximize your 401(k) contributions and take full advantage of your employers match. Next, you should start adding to your IRA account as much as possible. There is a maximum amount, which is presently $4,000 for those under 55. You and your spouse are each eligible. Then if you still have money available, you should open your own investment savings account. An initial investment of as little as $100 is all that's required to get your savings/investment plan started. Try to put away as much money as you are able. However, don't build your credit card debt to add to your account. You will be running up credit card bills and in effect borrowing money from your credit card at an interest rate that is higher than what you could ever earn. The more frequently you contribute, the faster your savings will grow through the magic of compounding. Remember, you'll need discipline since there is never a shortage of things to buy.

7.5 Retire a Millionaire

The following table illustrates how much you need to save each month to accumulate $500,000, $1 million or $2 million in savings by age 65. These would be a combination of company 401(k), personal and spousal IRAs, and personal savings.

At age 25 and 35, you're likely starting from scratch. At ages 45 and 55 the table assumes you already have money in savings. The amounts selected will of course vary for each employee. The table is based on earning 8% annually (tax deferred).

AGE	Savings at Start	Goal	Required Monthly Savings
25	$ 0	$ 500,000	$ 150
	$ 0	$ 1,000,000	$ 300
	$ 0	$ 2,000,000	$ 600
35	$ 0	$ 500,000	$ 338
	$ 0	$ 1,000,000	$ 676
	$ 0	$ 2,000,000	$ 1,352
45	$ 50,000	$ 500,000	$ 450
	$ 50,000	$ 1,000,000	$ 1,276
	$ 50,000	$ 2,000,000	$ 2,921
55	$ 100,000	$ 500,000	$ 1417
	$ 100,000	$ 1,000,000	$ 3,917
	$ 100,000	$ 2,000,000	$ 8,942

The above table illustrates how it only requires modest but regular saving to reach a very substantial nest egg. For example a 45 year old only needs to save $1,276 per month to reach $1,000,000 at age 65. For many this amount can be satisfied from their company sponsored 401 (k) alone.

The table also illustrates how it becomes more difficult to accumulate the wealth needed for retirement when you start late. Conversely, starting young will make it much easier to accumulate the money necessary. Starting at age 25 or 35 makes it relatively easy to reach your goals. So, once again the message is clear—**START TODAY!**

Don't be concerned if you do not have the "savings at the start" indicated in the table above. That shouldn't prevent you from doing all you can to accumulate the monthly savings needed to eventually make you a millionaire. Remember it's hard to predict how much money you will need for retirement. The key is to accumulate as much as you can. Having money to leave your heirs is nothing to be ashamed of.

The previous chapters focused on reducing waste and accumulating wealth. Managing your nest egg is not a simple proposition. The next chapters will address how to manage your funds to optimize growth without excessive risk.

Chapter 8

Managing Your Money

The previous chapters focused on controlling spending so that you can begin to save and start to build your nest egg. This chapter will begin to address putting your money to work for you to build wealth.

There are a number of ways to invest money including real estate, artwork, private business, collectibles, gold, etc. But there are five places that most workers typically invest their money:

1. Workplace tax deferred investment accounts
2. Personal tax deferred investment accounts
3. Your own personal investments
4. Certificates of deposit and government bonds
5. Personal savings and checking accounts

Everyone needs to have some money readily available to cover emergencies such as loss of a job or a major medical expense beyond that covered by health insurance. The remainder needs to go into investments. The investment alternatives are listed above in the normal order of priority for most people (excluding those particularly risk averse). You should first maximize the workplace tax deferred accounts which includes 401(k) plans for most workers, 403(b) for non-profit organizations and educators, 457 plans for government workers, or Keogh plans for self-employed individuals. The next step is to contribute to a personal tax-deferred account sometimes referred to as an IRA or Individual Retirement Account. Both items 1 and 2 limit the amount you can contribute by law since they are tax-deferred.

Once the limits for the first two are reached, your savings should then be put into item 3, personal or joint investment accounts. Items 4 and 5, certificates of deposit, savings accounts, or government bonds should be reserved for particularly risk-averse individuals but can be utilized for your emergency funds. Another investment choice sometimes considered is a personal annuity, which is really an insurance policy more than an investment vehicle.

8.1 Pre-Tax Accounts

How can you put your money to work for you? The best way is to maximize the use of "other people's money". In this case "other people" refers to the Federal Government and your employer.

The Federal Government allows (even encourages) you to put away money for your retirement. The money grows tax-free in work place pre-tax (also called tax-advantaged) investments like 401(k), 403(b), or Keogh plans as well as Individual Retirement Accounts (IRAs). The inducement for you is that they do not tax the portion of your salary deposited into these accounts or the profit on the accounts until withdrawal many years later.

In addition, many company savings plans offer an employer match which could be anywhere from 2% to 8% of your salary if you participate in their plan. Therefore, you get both the benefit of an employer match as well as saving and investing the would-be income tax on a portion of your salary for many years. Hence you are also using the government's portion to invest. The money can grow tax-free until withdrawal upon retirement at which time you will then pay tax on the money. Keep in mind that there are penalties for early withdrawal.

How much of a difference does the tax-deferral make? The Table below illustrates the advantages to an individual who invests $10,000 every year in a tax-deferred plan.

- Without a tax-advantaged fund, the $10,000 of income will be taxed. It might only leave $7,000 per year for you to invest. Investing the $7,000 every year for 25 years at 8 % return would result in $511,000 after 25 years, a sizeable sum.
- Now let's assume that you can invest the whole $10,000 each year since the income is not subject to taxes. At an 8 % growth rate you will have $731,000 or nearly a quarter million dollars more.
- Now if you have an employer's match of say an additional $3,000 per year, you would have a total account valued at $950,000. This nearly doubles the $511,000 the same $10,000/yr could grow into without a tax-advantaged fund. Pretty good deal, wouldn't you say?

	Annual Contribution	Amount Invested After Taxes	Value After 25 years @ 8% return	Amount with 3% employer match
No Tax-advantage	$10,000	$ 7,000	$ 511,000	N/A
Tax-advantage	$10,000	$10,000	$ 731,000	$ 950,000

You need to be aware that tax-advantaged accounts typically restrict your use of the money before you reach retirement age (usually age 59 ½). However, the 2001 tax law expands the use of tax-advantaged accounts to pay for your child's or a dependent's college expenses.

8.2 Workplace 401(k) Plans

History lesson—Years ago employers provided pensions, promising employees a regular paycheck at the end of their working years. Employers had to set aside enough money for each employee, and invest it wisely to assure that there would be adequate funds available for the number of years of the employee's (and their spouse's) retirement. But this turned out to be a rather daunting task for many companies. Saving enough and investing right wasn't easy for many companies who often left pensions only partially funded. Meeting these obligations turned out to be a serious financial burden on the company. So it is no wonder that employers were anxious to get out from under further pension responsibility.

In 1978, Congress decided that Americans needed some encouragement to save more money for retirement. They thought that if they gave people a way to save for retirement with the inducement of lowering their state and federal taxes that people would take advantage. The Tax Reform Act included a section authorizing the creation of tax-deferred savings plans for employees. The plan got its name from its section number and paragraph in the Internal Revenue Code—**Section 401, paragraph (k).**

With the advent of the 401(k), companies were able to shift the responsibility of funding retirement from the employers to the rank-and-file workers. Suddenly, it would be the employee who had to figure out how much money to save from every paycheck and how to invest it so there would be an adequate nest egg stashed away once he/she stopped working.

What makes a 401(k) different from other retirement plans? A number of things differentiate a 401(k) plan from other retirement plans.

- These are defined contribution plans. When you participate in a 401(k) plan, you decide how much money you want to contribute to your account. You can usually put up to 15 percent of your salary into the account on a monthly basis. Yet the employer still has the right to limit that amount. The IRS limits your total annual contribution to $15,500 (for 2007) plus an additional $5,000 catch-up contribution for workers over 50 years of age. There are other limits for "highly compensated" employees.
- The money you contribute comes out of your pay *before* taxes are calculated, and more importantly, before you ever have a chance to get your hands on it. That makes the 401(k) one of the most painless ways to save for retirement.
- If you're lucky, your employer will match a portion of your contribution. The matched amount they offer is an added incentive for you to participate. The catch is that the employer typically doesn't put anything

in unless you do. If you aren't participating in the program, you're basically leaving money on the table that you could use for your retirement.
- The 401(k) money is given to a third party administrator who invests it in mutual funds, bonds, money market accounts, etc. The third party doesn't determine the mix of investments—you do. The administrator usually has a list of investment vehicles you can choose from as well as providing some guidelines for the level of risk you may be taking. Some even offer free investment advice.

The 401(k) in practice—The concept of a 401(k) sounded simple enough. The government, which didn't want people to depend solely on Social Security when they retired, would give people an incentive to save. Each person with a 401(k) or similar work place retirement plan (457 plan for government workers or 403(b) plans for nonprofit organizations) would get an upfront tax break if the employee would place the funds in a workplace savings plan. The intent was for the worker to invest the money and leave it there to grow until they retired. Remember "the magic of compounding".

But it didn't turn out as hoped. Employees once again are demonstrating that many can't, or won't, manage their own money. About three decades into the retirement-saving experiment, Americans are struggling with the responsibility of planning for their future. About 1/3 of workers do not participate in their employers 401(k) plans and 20% of those enrolled do not contribute enough to get the full employers match. Only around 10% contribute the maximum to these plans. Younger workers in their 20s are so out touch with the concept of saving that about half of them don't bother to enroll in 401(k) plans at all, even passing up free money from their employers. Even if money is tight, it is hoped that one would contribute at least enough to get the company's full match.

Companies are now compensating by moving toward automatic enrollment. This requires the employee to opt out in order to <u>avoid</u> participation. Fortunately very few opt out after being automatically enrolled in their workplace plans. More than half of U.S. companies participated in automatically enrolling workers in 2007. This plan also includes enrolling workers over 50 in the $5,000 catch-up contribution in addition to the $15,500 maximum. Very few would have taken advantage of the $5,000 catch-up contribution without the auto-enrollment feature.

Unfortunately many workers do not take advantage of the portable nature of their 401(k) plan. They use their 401 (k) as a temporary savings fund and cash out when leaving their job instead of rolling the funds into another tax-deferred plan like an IRA. With the number of job changes the average worker will go through, cashing out their plans will prevent them from adequately building their savings.

Taking Maximum Advantage of the 401(k)—The main feature of 401(k) investing is the act of saving regularly and this is done automatically before the employee can spend the money. Some think 401(k) success is all about selecting funds with hot performance. In reality, how much you save on a regular basis matters far more than what your funds return.

Suppose you started work in 1990 with a $40,000 salary. If you saved just 2% of your pay but were such a brilliant investor that you put your 401(k) into top-returning funds every year with a return of 10%, you would have finished 2005 with nearly $28,000 in your 401(k). Now suppose you were clueless about investing, picked mediocre funds year after year that paid only 5%, but were frugal enough to save a full 6% of your salary. You'd end up with nearly $54,000 in 2005. That's right: nearly twice as much as the brilliant investor. Frugal savers generally outperform brilliant investors.

A growing number of employers will automatically sign employees up for their company's 401(k), as well as regularly increase their contributions, making saving literally effortless. The problem is that these automatic investments often start at just 2% to 3% of your salary. This is not enough. You should figure on putting away as much as possible. Put away at least 6 % of your salary or even more if your employer doesn't match your savings. Then try to increase your 401(k) contributions annually until you reach the maximum allotted. If you're currently on track to do so, congratulations—you're accomplishing something the vast majority of Americans can't or won't do.

If you're starting late (already in your 50's) it is important to maximize your contributions. Investing the maximum of $ 20,500 (for workers over 50) for 15 years can grow to $716,000 at a 10% return, even without an employer match. Now you're catching up in a hurry.

One thing to remember about the contributions your employer makes is that it doesn't count toward the total annual amount you can contribute ($15,500 in 2007). However the IRS limits the total annual amount the employer can contribute.

Drawbacks to the 401(k)—If you withdraw your money before you are 59.5 years old, you'll generally have to pay the tax on the withdrawal, **PLUS** a 10% penalty to the IRS. However, if you are at least 55 when you leave your job, you can take distributions from your 401(k) without paying a penalty (but you will still owe income taxes on your withdrawals). Keep your money in your employer's plan when you leave the job or retire early if you plan to withdraw some of the funds before age 59 ½. If you transfer it to an IRA, you'll lose the "55-and-out" option.

Often there is a vesting schedule associated with the employer contributions to your 401(k). Vesting means that there is a tiered schedule for transferring full ownership of the employer's contributions to you. For example, one's employer may have a three-year vesting schedule that increases your ownership of the employer's share of the money by one-third each year. After three years, the money all belongs to the employee as will all future employer contributions.

Some companies require the company match portion to be invested in company stock. Even this can usually be moved out of company stock once an employee reaches 50 years of age. The company's stock contribution is still better than not receiving the company match at all. But you should minimize the investment of your portion of the fund into company stock. There have been too many horror stories in recent years of companies going bankrupt or near bankrupt and employee stockholders losing their life savings. Can you spell ENRON? How about BEAR STEARNS?

How safe is your money?—What if your employer declares bankruptcy? How do you know your money is safe? The Employment Retirement Income Security Act (ERISA) that was passed in 1974, includes regulations that protect your retirement account. It requires that all 401(k) deposits be held in custodial accounts in order to keep your money safe in the event that something happens to your employer. In other words, the company does not control your 401(k) plan.

ERISA also sets requirements that must be followed, such as sending you regular account statements, providing easy access to your account, and maintaining compliance so that the plan is fair to everyone in the company. It also requires that your employer provide access to informative information about the investment options within your plan. These options can no longer be limited to company stock but must provide a large choice of investments options managed by major investment companies.

What if you change employers?—The worst mistake you can make is to cash out your 401(k) and spend the money. Not only will you end up losing much of your savings to taxes and penalties, but you'll also set back your retirement savings. Instead, pick one of these three options.

1) Roll the money into your new employer's 401(k)
Do this if you like your new plan's low costs and investment options. It will also help keep your retirement money in fewer places, making it easier to manage.

2) Continue your old 401(k)
Go with this option if you like the funds you already picked and are confident you can keep tabs on an account from a place you no longer work. Remember that the new employer's plans probably offer very similar options.

3) Rollover the 401(k) Account into your own IRA Account
Choosing this option allows you the freedom to invest with nearly any mutual fund company, bank or stock brokerage. You will still need to track both your IRA and your new employer's 401(k).

How to transfer an account: Call the investment company of your choice, and then sit back and let things happen for you. Most major firms will do the paperwork and send it to you for your signature. Really, it's that easy.

What is a 403(b) Plan?—A 403(b) plan, which is also known as a tax-sheltered annuity (TSA) plan is a retirement plan for employees of public schools and certain tax-exempt organizations. Individual accounts in a 403(b) plan can be custodial accounts invested in mutual funds or annuity contracts provided through an insurance company. They offer the same advantages as 401(k) accounts.

8.3 Personal Tax Deferred Accounts

Once you have maximized your 401(k) (or 403b) plan contributions (or if you have no access to a 401(k) or 403(b) plan) you should then start contributing to Individual Retirement Accounts (IRAs). Remember that you can contribute to both a 401(k) as well as an IRA. You should open an IRA even if you have very little money left over after your 401(k) contributions. Ultimately you want to contribute the maximum to both your 401(k) and your IRA.

What is an IRA? It is a personal retirement savings plan available to anyone who receives taxable compensation during the year. There are two types of IRAs, known as Roth IRAs and Traditional IRAs. Both are widely considered the most beneficial retirement savings vehicle available after an employer-sponsored retirement plan such as a 401(k).

Income required for IRA eligibility includes wages, tips, bonuses, commissions, and even taxable alimony. Husbands and wives may each have an IRA, even if one person in the marriage has no personal earned income. Each person's annual IRA contribution is limited to $5,000 each (in 2008), plus another $1,000 for people 50 and older. So you and your wife can collectively invest $10,000 (or $12,000 if over 50) tax-deferred. This immediately saves you the tax you would have to pay on this sum of earnings (for a conventional IRA). Depending on your tax bracket, it could be like putting $3,500 in after-tax money into savings and actually having $5,000 in your account earning additional money for you.

When a couple's adjusted gross income (AGI) reaches $156,000, deductibility for such contributions begins to decline, and it reaches zero at a joint AGI of $166,000 (if filing jointly). The AGI phase out begins at $83,000 and is completed at $103,000 for the individual earner. A Roth IRA has slightly higher phase out limits ($99,000 to $ 114,000)

What if your company doesn't offer a 401(k)? Or even if they do—An IRA is the logical next step after maximizing your 401(k). It can help expand your retirement planning options beyond what is offered in your 401(k). Either a Roth or Traditional IRA will:

- Offer a broader range of investment choices than your employer-sponsored retirement plan including your choice of mutual funds, stocks, bonds, treasuries, CDs, annuities, etc.
- Help you enjoy more tax savings with the potential of tax-free withdrawals (Roth IRA) or tax-deferred contributions (Traditional IRA) in addition to the tax advantage of your 401(k).

You can even enroll in an automatic IRA investing plan at any number of major mutual funds or brokerage firms. The idea is simple—you open an account and agree to have a specified amount of money transferred each month from your checking account into the mutual fund. Some mutual funds let you launch an automatic investing plan with as little as $50. In other cases, you might have to meet a minimum initial investment requirement, which can vary from $50 to $3,000 or so. Once you set up the account, the money moves from your checking account to your mutual fund account like clockwork, without you having to do a thing. As your paycheck grows, it's a good idea to boost the amount you invest as well (until you reach the annual allowance). This way, your savings will keep pace with your expanding income, increasing the odds that you'll be able to retire without having to seriously ratchet back your lifestyle. Just be careful that you don't end up with additional credit card debt as a result of withdrawing too much money from your checking account.

There are so many mutual fund families available today to handle your personal IRA plan. You should consider the major no-load (no fee to open an account) funds like Vanguard, T. Rowe Price, and Fidelity along with many others. These mutual fund families will offer investment guidance to help lead you through the maze of options. They will all be glad to help you get started. Your employer's 401(k) plan will typically designate the family of funds to be utilized for their sponsored 401(k) plan. You should consider setting up your IRA with the same family of funds that are used for your 401(k). They will be kept in separate accounts.

Types of IRAs—The two most popular types of IRAs are Roth and traditional IRAs. But there are others as well.

- **Traditional IRA**
  A traditional IRA allows one's retirement savings to grow tax-deferred. The income placed in an IRA is not subject to income tax for that year. Anyone under the age of 70½ with earned income can invest in a traditional IRA. A non-working spouse may also be eligible to make contributions depending upon earned income levels. For 2008, you can invest up to $6,000 in a Traditional IRA if you are 50 or over, or $5,000 if you are under age 50.

- **Roth IRA**
  A Roth IRA is available to anyone at any age and also allows his/her earnings to grow tax-free. Although the contributions are not tax-

deductible, contributions to a Roth IRA can be withdrawn at any time without being subject to penalty or tax. Earnings are free from federal tax if they are withdrawn after age 59½ provided the account has been open for more than 5 years.

- **SEP IRA—Simplified Employee Pension**
  This is an employer established and funded Simplified IRA for self-employed individuals and small businesses. The employer or employee can put up to 25% (but no more than $45,000 for 2007) of his compensation into the special IRA account. Sole proprietors may establish these plans for their own benefit. They are sometimes used instead of Keogh retirement plans because they have fewer administrative and tax filing requirements.

- **SIMPLE IRA**
  A SIMPLE (Savings Incentive Match Plan for Employees) IRA plan is an IRA-based plan that gives small employers (100 or less employees) a simplified method to make contributions toward their employees' retirement as well as the owners' own retirement. Under a SIMPLE IRA plan, employees may choose to make salary reduction contributions (tax-deferred) up to 3% with the employer making matching contributions. The attractive features of this plan includes not only the ability for the employer to establish and fund a retirement plan for the benefit of his/her employees, but it also permits employees to contribute up to $10,500 per year (with an additional $2,500 catch up contribution for those over 50 years of age) into an IRA.

- **KEOGH PLANS**
  A KEOGH PLAN is for self employed people and business owners. If one is the owner of a self-employed business, he/she can generally deduct the entire amount of yearly Keogh contribution (including contributions made on the employees' behalf). If one is a partner in a self-employed business, he/she can deduct the amount contributed by the partnership on the partner's behalf. Contributions to a Keogh are made pre-tax, which reduces the taxable income. The interest, dividends, and capital gains earned on Keogh money also grow tax-deferred. Like a traditional IRA, withdrawing funds must start at age 70 ½ at which time they will be taxed.

- **TRADITIONAL NONDEDUCTIBLE IRA**
  For completeness it is pointed out that there is a traditional nondeductible IRA, but the contributor won't realize tax benefits comparable to those available through Roth or traditional tax-deductible IRAs. Since a very high income will prohibit one from making contributions to tax deductible IRAs, a traditional nondeductible IRA may be attractive because of the tax-deferred growth.

The Roth versus Traditional IRA—Roth IRAs were enacted into law in 1997 some 23 years after the Employee Retirement Income Security Act (ERISA) created traditional IRAs. About 30% of U.S. households owned a traditional IRA in 2006 versus about 13% who owned a Roth IRA.

The Roth IRA differs from the traditional IRA in the way it treats taxes. With a traditional IRA, you invest income that won't be taxed, which reduces your tax bite for the year, but then have your withdrawals (typically after age 59 ½) taxed. Still, this is a great deal. But with a Roth IRA, you invest money after it has already been taxed so you get no immediate tax benefit, but ultimately get to make withdrawals tax-free. That can be a big advantage since the dividends and appreciation on the account are never taxed and your investments have a longer time to grow since there is no required withdrawal age. It is also advantageous if your tax bracket after retirement will still be high.

Choose a Roth IRA if you can do without the tax break right now. It's a more flexible instrument, for the following reasons:

- It allows you to withdraw your contributions at any time, penalty and tax-free.
- You do not have to take mandatory distributions at age 70 1/2.

Choose a traditional IRA if you need that tax deduction right now, or you anticipate paying taxes at a significantly lower rate in retirement when, for most retirees, their income is much lower. Keep in mind that many people fear that tax rates may need to rise in the future because we have a multitude of financial crises such as health care, 78 million aging baby boomers, and the death of defined-benefit pensions. Somebody's going to have to pay for this. We might now have the lowest tax rates we'll ever see in our lifetime. On the other hand there are proposals out there like the fair tax, the flat tax, and the national sales tax. What if one of those is passed? Looking forward 30 years, who knows what the tax situation is going to look like?

IRA Withdrawals—There is a penalty for withdrawals prior to age 59 ½. Mandatory withdrawals (for traditional IRAs) must begin no later than April 1 of the year following the year the IRA owner reaches age 70 1/2. Failure to take required minimum distributions at that age results in a 50% excise tax on the amounts not distributed. Roth IRAs are not tax-deferred and as such have no mandatory distribution requirement.

Money may be withdrawn from an IRA at any time, but on withdrawal it may be taxed and penalized. Withdrawals from a traditional IRA prior to age 59 1/2 will result in a 10% excise tax as well as the ordinary income tax. Withdrawals after age 59 ½ will be taxed at ordinary income tax rates. Roth IRA withdrawals have the special benefit that there are no income taxes or early withdrawal penalties since the funds placed in the account have already been taxed.

8.4 Personal Investment Accounts

Further Savings beyond the IRA—Once you have taken maximum advantage of your 401(k) and IRA, it is a good idea to open a joint account with your spouse to accumulate additional savings. You can contribute on a month-to-month basis or periodically. By investing monthly regardless of whether the stock market is headed up or down, you eliminate the trap that so many investors fall into. Too many try to time their investments so that they get in before the market soars and try to get out just before the market tanks. People who try to engage in this sort of timing often end up plowing large sums of money into an investment at a bad time or end up being paralyzed by indecision and not investing it at all. It is better to just keep shoveling it in a little at a time. This way, you buy at a variety of prices, reducing the risk that you'll invest it all at once just as the market is ready to tank.

Historically, personal investing in stock mutual funds has performed far better than putting your money into fixed investments like a savings account, bonds, or certificates of deposit. Despite the occasional setbacks, the market has continued to rise over the long run. That is not to say that you can't actually lose money on stocks in the future. Buying into the market with a large sum as the market approaches a historical high may end up costing you in the long run. And as the investment firms always point out "Past performance is no guarantee of future performance". We will devote a later chapter explaining the risk and potential rewards associated with stock market investing.

Do not feel intimidated by the thought of personally selecting stocks and selling them at the appropriate time. This is no longer the preferred approach for stock market investing. There are much easier ways to invest. The mutual fund companies have simplified the whole process for the small investor. They select the stocks and other investments for you, diversify the accounts, and do all the accounting. They even send you a single statement at the end of the year informing you which figures need to be included in your tax return. And for all this their fee is generally less than a paid investment specialist.

8.5   Certificates of Deposit and Government Bonds

Our grandparents knew of only two ways to save. They put their money in passbook savings accounts or purchased government bonds. Passbook savings accounts were a good way of accumulating money for a major purchase like a television set or a car. The interest earned was a minor feature and generally didn't keep pace with inflation. Government bonds were intended for long-term holdings like saving for a child's education. Hence it was not unusual to give bonds as gifts for children's birthdays or for weddings.

CD and bond rates tend to be very close to inflation rates. It becomes a challenge to beat inflation with your taxable CDs or government bonds (government bonds are usually exempt from state taxes but subject to federal taxes). But on the other hand the principle and interest are practically guaranteed.

Today you can purchase certificates of deposit (CDs) that give higher interest rates. In some cases close to what corporate bonds offer. CDs can be purchased through your local bank. The interest rate is much higher than a typical passbook savings or checking account at your bank but far from the historical returns that people have been getting from common stock investments. It's generally accepted that investing in the stock market is an effective way to stay ahead of inflation while CDs and government bonds are not.

However many people have a low tolerance for risk and do not have the fortitude to live with the ups and downs that are common with the stock market. Bonds and CDs are the preferred route for those who can't sleep at night with the wild ride from stocks.

What are CDs?—CDs are certificates of deposit that banks offer in various denominations and for different durations. The CD locks in, and guarantees, the interest rate for the full term of the CD. The CDs with longer durations (like 5 years) will have a somewhat higher interest rate than those with shorter durations (like 3 months). The difference may be only in the range of 1% between a 3-month and 5-year CD. CDs often offer higher rates than government bonds.

The main concern with short term CDs is that the offered interest rate on new CDs can drop before you have a chance to renew. Hence you would get less interest on the next CD you purchase after the first one expires. This makes it difficult to predict how much cash flow you will acquire by purchasing these. Longer term CDs are advisable when interest rates are generally dropping and shorter term CDs are preferred when they are rising. This is why many CD owners are keeping a close eye on the statements from the Federal Reserve whose actions impact future interest rates. It should be noted that there is a substantial penalty for cashing in a CD before expiration.

Government bonds are one of the world's largest and most liquid markets. They are used to finance the Federal government's debt. The bonds, issued by the U.S. Treasury and other U.S. government agencies, are considered to have the bond market's lowest risk because they are guaranteed by the U.S. government's "full faith and credit" or, in other words, its taxing authority.

Government agencies and government-sponsored enterprises such as Ginnie Mae (GNMA), Fannie Mae (FNMA) and Freddie Mac also issue debt to support their role in financing mortgages that enable more Americans to own homes. Their securities are also popular investments because of their high credit ratings.

Government bonds generally have a fixed rate of return although there are some that fluctuate periodically with the inflation rate. The duration of government bonds can be up to 30 years and most can be cashed in much earlier with no penalty, provided they are held for a minimum number of years. The bonds can be purchased directly from the government through their web site www.treasurydirect.gov where the latest rate and details of each type of offering is explained. Some of the more popular offerings include:

- **Treasury Bills**—Sometimes called T-Bills, these are sold in terms ranging from a few days to 26 weeks. They are sold at a discount from their face value. For instance, you might pay $970 for a $1,000 T-Bill. When the T-Bill matures, you would be paid $1,000. The difference between the purchase price and face value is interest.
- **Treasury Notes**—Sometimes called T-Notes, earn a fixed rate of interest paid every six months until maturity. Notes are issued in terms of 2, 5, and 10 years.
- **Treasury Bonds**—Pay a fixed rate of interest every six months until they mature. They are issued in a term of 30 years. They are auctioned four times a year, in February, May, August, and November for $1,000 minimum.
- **TIPS**—Treasury Inflation-Protected Securities provide protection against inflation. The principal of a TIPS changes with the inflation rate as measured by the Consumer Price Index (CPI), The investor is paid the adjusted principal or original principal, whichever is greater, when the TIPS mature. TIPS pay interest twice a year.
- **EE Savings Bonds** are a secure savings product that pays interest based on current market rates for up to 30 years. Electronic EE Savings Bonds are sold at face value directly from the U.S. Treasury (www.treaurydirect.gov). Paper EE Savings Bonds are sold at 1/2 of face value.
- **I Bonds** are a low-risk, liquid savings product. While one owns them they earn interest and protect against inflation. They come in small to large denominations of $50, $75, $100, $200, $500, $1,000, $5,000, and $10,000. The maximum allowed annual purchase is $30,000 per individual.

Corporate Bonds—These differ from Government Bonds and CDs in that they are sold on the open market and not directly back to the issuer. In this way the value of the bonds can change as interest rates change. The market price of the bond will decrease as general interest rates increase since it is possible to get a better interest rate on newer bonds (or CDs) while the interest rate on the existing bond is locked in for a period of time. Conversely, the value of bonds on the open market can increase as interest rates drop. Although bonds do not change in value as fast as stocks, they are still subject to changes in the market as well.

Unlike CDs and Government Bonds, corporate bonds do not need to be purchased directly. They can be purchased through a mutual fund account.

As a matter of fact, most diversified plans include a significant percentage of holdings in corporate bonds. We will explore this more fully in later chapters.

8.6 Tying it All Together

As previously stated, the path to riches is to maximize tax-deferred investments and then keep contributing to your own personal investment funds. Although it is not necessary for each account to be totally diversified, your overall holdings need to be. None of your accounts should be looked upon in isolation from your other accounts since the objective is to properly allocate and diversify the sum total of all your investments. For this reason your personal investments need to be integrated with the investments you've chosen for your 401(k) and IRA accounts. The purpose and advantages of diversification will be explored more fully in the next chapter.

Financial advisers will tell you that you should have a certain percentage of your holdings liquid (meaning able to convert to cash in an emergency). Although this is true, since you never know when you may be unemployed for 6 months, you still need to be somewhat aggressive with part of your holdings to stay ahead of inflation. The methods to accomplish this will be described in the next chapters.

Chapter 9

Investing Your Money

Previous chapters have focused on reducing waste to eliminate debt, while taking advantage of "other people money" through tax-deferred savings and employer matches. Once you begin to reduce waste, you will see, as a result, that there is indeed money available to put away for your future. The next step is to appropriately invest the money that you have put away. The challenge comes when you have to learn how to manage and let this money grow, taking advantage of the miracle of compounding. We will begin this chapter by looking at ways to manage your money.

9.1 Managing Your Own Money

In many ways, managing money is more of a challenge than reducing waste because managing large quantities of money is a completely foreign concept to many people. It doesn't just come naturally, either. Learning how to effectively manage your money will take many years and much time and research. You will need to live through some good and some poor financial markets to truly learn how they can affect your investments.

Hardly anyone took a class in school in money management. Nor is it something you can readily learn on the streets or at work from your friends and coworkers. Be careful, for there are many "experts" glad to give you the benefit of their experience. Your friends will brag of their prowess in smart investing. You will be tempted to treat their words as gospel while you struggle to learn new concepts. These "experts" sound awfully knowledgeable and utilize words to describe concepts that you have not encountered before.

Listening to some of these "experts" is a lot like listening to gamblers who brag about how much money they won at the racetrack or casino. It sounds like they always win. But they can't win all the time or they would all be rich and the gambling houses would go bankrupt. You just know that's never going to happen. You need to avoid getting roped into the old axiom that "in the land of the blind, the one-eyed man is king". In the case of money management, the "one-eyed man" could cause you to lose a lot of money.

Where does the learning begin? It starts with taking the time to read and ask questions until you understand the basics of investing, meanwhile taking an active role in managing your tax-deferred accounts. The mutual fund company that manages your employer-sponsored 401(k) will provide some support for you. They will explain and guide you through the basics, but will not give you definitive advice on your personal situation. They can be a great sounding board that will listen to your plans and comment on whether your choices make sense or whether there are other factors you are missing. They will not make the choice for you. You can contact them and ask questions that can lead you to make reasonable choices for your investments.

Your company sponsored 401(k) plan likely offers a number of different options through a major mutual fund. The offerings typically vary from conservative investments like bonds and treasury bills all the way up to a basket of stocks of established companies. The blends of common stocks can include a whole host of large, long established companies (called blue chip companies), as well as large established technology companies and well-known foreign companies. Employer sponsored plans often do not permit the very riskiest investments such as a basket of newly created foreign technology companies when it comes to your tax-deferred program.

Mutual fund companies can also provide you with a table qualitatively rating the relative risk inherent in each type of investment that they offer, so that you can better appreciate the risk you would be taking. You generally will want to start with a relatively low risk blend of securities. Once you observe the performance of your fund(s) and make adjustments, you will begin feeling comfortable taking greater risks. In this way, you will learn to handle your own investments over time and also to evaluate results by professionals.

9.2 Professional Investment Advice

There are many licensed professional investment advisors out there who are more than willing to manage your money. After all that's how they make a living. The credible professional planners are classified as Certified Professional Financial Planners (CFP) who generally have the best training and credentials. Chartered Financial Consultants (ChFC) are planners who utilize insurance vehicles to reach goals. Personal Financial Specialists (PFS) are certified public accountants. All three have been formally trained and passed difficult certification exams.

Professional Planners differ from "investment advisors" in that they review your overall financial situation including spending and insurance needs as well your tolerance for risk to determine how best to invest your money. Professional planners are compensated in a variety of ways. Most tend to charge you about 1% of your account every year to manage your money while some will work for an hourly charge in lieu of charging a set percentage. Professional planners tend to create a diverse portfolio based on what he/she feels is in your best long-term interest. Professionals do not focus on "quick hits" and do not trade very often or try to time the market. They will also inform you when it is the proper time to sell a particular holding. There are some that will even do the trading for you.

There are many other types of investment advisors around. They are trained and licensed to trade stocks and manage and invest other people's money. They sometimes make their money by charging you a percentage of your annual profits instead of a percentage of the value of your account. They deal mostly in common stocks, buying and selling specific stocks and options. They are not usually concerned with fully diversifying your account, but look to buy the "hottest" sectors and specific stocks to make money rapidly. They will tend to inform you of the "glowing" record they have compiled over the past 20 years and how they've outperformed the investment community as well as their peers.

There is a group of advisors (commissioned planners and stockbrokers) who don't charge you any fee at all to manage your money. That sounds great—doesn't it? However, you probably can't afford these advisors. They make their money by commissions from the purchase you make under their direction. This could lead you to what are called "loaded" funds that charge you a commission to purchase the fund in addition to an annual charge to manage it. Part of this "load" goes to pay the advisor's commission. These advisors can be conflicted by the higher commissions they can earn as opposed to optimizing the return on your investment. The loaded funds generally perform similarly to the no-load (or no commission) funds and the annual operating costs are comparable as well. Despite having to pay a fee to join, many people have been quite satisfied with the results from loaded funds. This is perhaps because they don't realize that they might have fared just as well with no-load funds if only they could have personally been able to select the appropriate ones to purchase.

Most investment advisors consider themselves expert at selecting specific stocks. They feel they can build a diversified portfolio for you by only picking "the best" stocks. Many of them have a glowing record. Looking back on the historical returns that these advisors have been bragging about, you may feel very comfortable putting your money in their hands. Sounds good, doesn't it? But all that glitters is not gold. You should note that the stock market has done very well for most of the last 20 years, allowing these advisors to all look like geniuses. As a matter of fact, the most aggressive managers, putting their clients' money at the most risk, have generally performed the best. But were their actions truly in their clients' best interests?

Surveys taken to compare investment advisors against each other, and against mathematical chance, have proven quite interesting. As you might imagine, the advisors who invest heavily in aggressive stocks and mutual funds tend to outperform the indexes and overall averages when the stock market does very well. Conversely many aggressive advisors do quite poorly when the market tanks. The exact opposite is true of conservative investment professionals whose relative performance is better in a down market. Your tolerance for risk is an important factor in selecting an agent to represent you.

The ever-changing stock market makes it difficult to evaluate the advisors' performance. For example, the overall stock market could drop 3% in a poor (bearish) year and, through the efforts of your advisor, your investments could break even. While you may not be very happy with your return, you still did well utilizing this advisor. Paying a commission of only 1% instead of losing 3% will put you ahead (less losses). Alternatively, with a more aggressive money manager, your managed account could drop 6% in a bad year and you will be out an additional 1% for the commission, for a total of a 7% loss. Now you have something to complain about. Usually professional advisors do better in good years since they seem to recognize which areas of the market are growing long before the public becomes aware of it. You could get a 13% return in a year that the overall market rises 9%. In this case the 1% commission was well worthwhile.

So when analyzing your options, the questions you need to answer are as follows:

- Considering that the professionals have a mixed track record, what chance do you have investing alone?
- Are you capable of managing your own money?
- Is it worthwhile to pay 1% of your account every year for a management fee?
- Do you want to get more involved to learn how to appropriately handle your investments?

9.3 Risk

Unless you are just plain filthy rich to begin with, you will need to grow your wealth in order to have enough money for retirement. The relatively safe methods of saving such as CDs, savings accounts, bonds, and treasury bills can't provide enough income (especially after taxes) to beat inflation. Hence you will find your nest egg declining in value unless you take some risk by investing a good portion of your funds in common stocks, both domestic and foreign.

Professional financial planners, as well as some mutual fund companies, will encourage you to fill out a questionnaire to project how much money you will need in retirement, how much you will need to save, and how much return you will need on your investments to get to that point. These factors are interrelated since the more you want to have and the less you save will result in the need for more risk. The data you enter will serve as a guide for advising how much risk you will need to take to get the return you will need to meet your stated goals. Of course there is also a limit on how much risk you want to take.

As an example, if you have $300,000 already saved at age 50 and need to build it up to $1,000,000 at age 65, a financial advisor would calculate that you will need more than 8% return after taxes (or tax-deferred) assuming you are not adding ongoing funds to the account. If, however, you have no tolerance for risk and put your savings in bonds or CDs providing 4.5% return you will have far less (almost $400,000 less). That being said, you will not meet your goals. See the table below:

Amount Invested	Age	% Return	Final Amount
$ 300,000 in Stocks	50	8 (deferred or after taxes)	$ 952,000
$ 300,000 in Bonds	50	4.5	$ 580,000

These numbers can be very misleading since the $580,000 that the fund would reach with 4.5% return, will have roughly the same purchasing power as the $300,000 you started with after you pay taxes and suffer through 15 years of inflation. This is why most experts will tell you that some "reasonable" amount of risk is unavoidable. The question arises as to how aggressive and how much risk you should take? The more aggressive you are, the greater the chance that the opposite effect could occur—you could actually lose money instead of growing your nest egg.

Historically, the 8% return may seem reasonable without taking too much risk. However, it is seldom that straight forward. For if you want the account to grow to $1,000,000 of today's purchasing power, accounting for 15 years of inflation, you could require close to an 11% return. This is quite optimistic and would call for overly aggressive investing. The key term again is "aggressive". The more aggressive the investment, the more risk involved.

How are you supposed to know if your goals are simply too lofty? There is no really good answer to that question. The best approach is probably to take on some limited risk and continue to add to your account by saving more each month. The net effect is that you may need to reduce your retirement goals. Remember for those who like sleeping well at night, less risk might be the way to go.

Let's learn more about **different types of RISK**. How can you get burned? Let us count the ways.

- **Business Risk**—A company may fail, leaving the stock or bond you hold worthless. This problem was more pronounced when people had most of their stock holdings tied up in one company, frequently their employer. Conventional wisdom now frowns on this practice.
- **Market Risk**—Even if you purchase stock in a strong company, a declining market may carry your stock, and most others, down. This is perhaps the greatest risk to your portfolio since a down, or "bear" market tends to take most stocks down with it. This is why diversification into different market sectors is essential.
- **Interest Rate Risk**—The value of stocks, bonds, and real estate varies with interest rates. Rising interest rates are usually bad for stocks, real estate, and existing corporate bonds. Higher interest rates, on the other hand, could be beneficial for CDs, short-term treasury notes and government bonds. Declining interest rates are usually good for stocks and corporate bonds as well as real estate (lower mortgage rate).

High interest rates can be difficult to recognize and the rates can change in a hurry. From 1981 to 1994, CD rates fell from a high of 17.27% to a low of 3.69%. In other words, income from CDs actually fell by 80%! In the 1980s, while CD rates were very high, the inflation rate was as high as most people can remember. The high CD rates in those days did not keep up with inflation on an after-tax basis. With the CD rates relatively low at the end of this period, investors actually came closer to keeping pace with the inflation rate. In other words they lost out less at the lower interest rates.

A popular approach for controlling interest rate risk is to arrange a bond (or CD) portfolio ladder so that the maturities are spread out over time. That way, a large portion of the bond portfolio is never cashed in or rolled over at any one time. But it is still very hard to keep up with inflation and taxes in this manner, much less build the true value of your nest egg.

- **Inflation Risk**—Your investments may not keep pace with inflation, resulting in a decrease in buying power. You can count on this being a major issue for essentially all retirees. Higher inflation rates tend to result in higher interest rates as the Federal Reserve tries to control inflation. But what seems like plenty of money today might prove inadequate 30 years in the future.
- **Currency Risk**—Foreign holdings change in value as the value of a currency changes. As the US dollar weakens, foreign goods and foreign travel become more expensive. Foreign stocks might fall if their exports to the U.S. drop off due to their higher prices from a weaker dollar. A weaker dollar makes U.S. exports less expensive on the world market, maintaining jobs that ship products overseas, reducing unemployment at home.
- **Political Risk**—The U.S. government may do something to affect the economic climate when a new President and Congress are elected. The impact of a new budget being put in place is always hard to predict. Factors like raising (or lowering) taxes or changing tax codes, declaring war, changes in health care, as well as changing the minimum wage can all affect the stock market very significantly.

The Danger of Eliminating Risk—Retirees, in the past, seemed to migrate to stable, low risk, investments to protect their nest egg since they were no longer employed and so could not make up for losses. Their investments typically returned very low rates, frequently below the actual inflation rate. Unfortunately we've learned over time that inflation can surely deplete the value of your nest egg very significantly. This effect becomes magnified by greater life expectancy, unless some degree of risk is accepted to compensate by achieving higher returns.

If today's retirees had purchased a diversified portfolio including U.S. stocks, foreign equities, as well as bonds and CDs during their working life, they would have much more money available for their retirement. Unfortunately, most were really not financially literate and so their fear of risk prevented them even looking to allocate their assets appropriately. To them, equities were risky, and CDs were safe! As you can see, this is not the whole story.

Most experts agree that it is inappropriate for long-term investors to place all or even most of their resources in safe investments like CDs, T-Bills and bonds. They feel that even retirees should only keep a portion of their wealth in these secure investments. The next chapter will explore strategies for investing your funds.

9.4 Overcoming Fear

The possibility of loss scares some folks out of investing in stocks since these will, at times, decline in value. The media is quick to report a seemingly unending litany of bad economic news including declining housing prices, ongoing sub-prime woes, a coming recession, a slowing economy, as well as a weakened dollar. It's natural for the investor to want to run for cover rather than endure a stomach-churning loss from which they may never recover.

Potential declines are unsettling for all investors, but even more so for those who are at, or nearing, the end of their careers. After all, the last thing you want is to see the money you've worked so hard for, saved so diligently and invested so carefully, get whacked with a big loss just when you're in the home stretch to retirement. But this isn't the time to give in to fear. Rather, it's a time to re-assess your investing strategy and consider what you need to do to remain on track toward a secure retirement. If you're like most people over 50, you probably have close to 10 years to work before you can retire. During that time, you've got to go through a bit of a balancing act. Your portfolio will need to include investments like stocks and mutual funds in order to provide returns that beat or at least keep pace with inflation.

On the one hand, you don't want to do anything to unduly jeopardize the savings that you have accumulated in 401(k) plans and other retirement accounts. But you still are faced with the need to make that money grow for many years. Remember, it's not as if you'll only be investing until age 65. After completing your career, you'll probably spend another 20 to 30 years in retirement during which you will want to continue to keep your money working for you. So even though your gut may be telling you otherwise, you don't want to minimize risk too much upon approaching retirement.

9.5 Saving, Speculating, and Investing

While most people understand that investing involves taking some risk with their money, they need to be aware that fluctuations in the financial markets and other risk factors as described above will sometimes cause declines in the value of their wealth. Remember that all investments involve some risk. But how much risk are you really taking? To gain some insight, consider the differences between saving, speculating, and investing.

Savings: Everybody needs to have some form of savings. This provides cash for emergencies such as loss of a job or large unexpected medical emergencies. It's also important to keep some ready cash available for paying tuition, taxes, vacations, or any major expenditures coming up in the next year or so. These savings can be in any form that can provide quick cash without forcing you to sell stocks at an inappropriate time. Types of savings normally include a bank savings or checking account, or better still a money market fund that provides higher interest rates and can still be converted to cash at a day's notice.

Both the principal and interest on bank deposits and CDs are guaranteed (within limits) by an agency of the federal government, the Federal Deposit Insurance Corporation (FDIC). Investment in a money market mutual fund, which is one of the safest investments, is not insured by any government agency. However, since money market funds are typically invested in U.S. Government backed securities, it is extremely unlikely that you will lose money.

Speculating: This is a polite name for gambling and although sometimes disguised as investing, has little in common with investing. There is certainly a lot of luck (usually bad) involved in these speculative practices. Bad things tend to happen when people take greater risks than they can afford, hoping to "get rich quick". Some common examples are:

- Purchasing a stock on a "hot tip" without understanding if it fits into your acceptable risk parameters
- Trying to time the stock market
- Day trading, hoping for small quick profits
- Limiting your investments to just a few stocks or specialized funds hoping to pick the right sectors (if you can)

Many people have made a lot of money by speculating, but many have also lost vast sums that they could not afford to lose. Speculation is certainly not for the unseasoned investor. Unfortunately, many new investors mistake one or more of these speculative practices for investing.

Investing is a thoughtful, prudent approach to money management. The investor understands that "slow and steady" wins the race and avoids speculative practices that can seriously hurt his/her nest egg. History has favored the long-term investor who holds their investments for years. An investor who takes the moderate risks necessary to achieve higher returns needs to be disciplined and careful in their approach. He needs to develop a plan geared towards one's goals, tolerance for risk, and current financial situation. It is important to adhere to a diversification plan, rather than chasing the hot new investments.

The speculative investor realizes that it's hard to sit calmly by the pool without a BlackBerry or laptop computer and a glass of scotch when one is constantly "playing" the stock market. A Savvy investor, on the other hand, know that jumping in and out of the market is one of the most counter-productive things that person can do. With a plan in place, he can put his investment program on autopilot, so it's less likely to get derailed by emotions, while trusting that the nest egg will grow appreciably in the coming years.

Investing in the present hot sector is a good way to lose. Many investors who try to do this end up out of sync with the winning sections of the market. Those who buy after the stock has already made most of it's gains often fall victim when the stock comes back down.

9.6 The Stock Market

It can be shown that the longer you hold your investments in the equity (stock) market, the better chance you have to smooth out market fluctuations. The educated stock market investor takes comfort from historical returns and doesn't overreact to the frequent swings in value.

The table below published by T. Rowe Price illustrates the volatility in stock market performance over the years. The best (and worst) 5, 10, and 20 year periods for the S&P (Standard and Poor's 500 largest U.S. Companies) Index are shown. It's interesting to note that the worst performing periods are back in the 1930's while some of the best performing periods are quite recent.

	Best Period	Worst Period
20 year period	1980-1999 17.9% annual return	1929-1948 3.1% annual return
10 year period	1949-1958 20.1 % annual return	1929-1938 0.9 % annual *loss*
5 year period	1995-1999 28.6 % annual return	1928-1932 12.5 % annual *loss*

Despite occasional setbacks, the U.S. stock market has continued to rise over the long run. In any 10-year period since 1926, you'd have made money in stocks 97 % of the time. Over any 20-year period you'd be ahead 100 % of the time. Sounds like you can't lose doesn't it? Not necessarily.

Of the three major asset classes—stocks, bonds, and cash investments—stocks have delivered the highest returns over the long run. That's why many long-term investors make stocks the largest portion of their portfolios. Those higher returns, however, come with significant risks.

Over the years, stock prices have skyrocketed—and plummeted—over relatively short periods. But over the long run, the upside has won out. While stocks as a whole have well outpaced inflation over very long periods, their tendency to suffer short-term declines has often kept investors confused and worried. Stocks are volatile by nature because they closely reflect the constantly changing overall economy and investor optimism as well as the prospects of the corporations that issue them.

Putting all your money into stocks when the market is at an all time high has not been a good strategy for success. After all, if the market tanks, as it did eight years ago, it could take you many years to break even. The best strategy for most people is to continuously invest money into the market as they save money and keep investing in a diversified program. The key word is **DIVERSIFIED**. A proven strategy is to decide on a mix of stocks and bonds that are likely to get you reasonable long-term growth without excessive risk and keep to it. The blend of stocks and bonds that's right for you will depend on a number of factors, including the size of your nest egg, your retirement goals, and your tolerance for risk. Another factor is the value of other resources you have to draw on including Social Security, a pension, home equity, cash value in life insurance policies, etc.

9.7 What is a Share of Stock?

A share of stock makes you an infinitesimal part owner in a corporation. This ownership gives you the right to share in that company's future financial performance, whether good or bad. When the company is doing well, it may pay out some of its profits by distributing dividends. On the other hand a company might choose to reinvest most of those profits in the hopes of increasing future sales, which in turn, may increase the value of your shares. The combination of dividends paid and changes in the stock price are the stock's total return.

The most lucrative feature of stocks over the years has been the increase in value as the company's profits rise, making the shares of stock more valuable. But there is always the risk of falling profits, or even losses, which will negatively impact the stockholder. When the company is doing poorly, dividend payments could shrink or disappear, and the value of your stock investment could drop or even be wiped out totally if the company goes bankrupt.

Income stocks are defined as stock in companies whose dividends are a large percentage of the total return to the investor. While **growth companies** pay very little in dividends, they put their profits back into growing the company, which hopefully has the effect of increasing the value of the stock.

9.8 What is a Mutual Fund?

Investors who have the time, money, knowledge, and inclination can build a portfolio one security at a time. But identifying, researching, and monitoring investments is beyond the capability of most people. Besides, to have a diversified stock portfolio would require investing in hundreds of companies to minimize the risk of a single company or industry falling on hard times. Each company would need to be carefully chosen to build a portfolio to include all major industries and variously sized companies. That's why most people prefer the convenience and instant diversification that mutual funds provide.

The idea behind a mutual fund is simple—Many people pool their money into a fund, which invests in various companies. When you buy stock in a company, you are buying a small part of the company. Owning mutual fund shares acts the same way. You own a small fraction of all the holdings within that mutual fund. The fund is managed by a professional money-manager who makes the decisions on what company and when to buy and later when to sell. The stock in each company within the portfolio fluctuates daily based on market gyrations affecting the value of each stock. The value of each share of the mutual fund varies in accordance with the value of the various holdings. Each investor shares proportionately in the fund's investment returns. The income (dividends) paid on the securities and any capital gains (or losses) caused by change in the price of securities the fund sells will be shared by all holders.

Let's examine the pros and cons of mutual fund investing.

Advantages—Mutual funds have become popular because they offer four main advantages:

- **Diversification**. A single mutual fund share can hold securities from hundreds or even thousands of corporations. This is far more than most investors could afford on their own. This diversification reduces the risk of a serious loss due to problems in a specific company or industry.
- **Professional management**. Few investors have the time or expertise to continuously manage their personal investments, to efficiently reinvest interest or dividend income, or to investigate the thousands of securities available in the financial markets. Mutual Funds have access to extensive research departments, market information, and skilled securities traders. An experienced advisor decides which securities to buy and sell for the fund.
- **Liquidity**. Shares in a mutual fund can be bought and sold on any business day, so investors have easy access to their money. The investor is cautioned not to take advantage of this feature to trade very often. In fact there are penalties for frequent trading. But the liquidity of the investor's funds makes them always available for unplanned emergencies.
- **Convenience**. Mutual funds offer services that make investing easier. Fund shares can be bought or sold by mail, telephone, or over the Internet. You can easily transfer your money from one mutual fund to another mutual fund as your financial needs change. You can even schedule automatic investments directly into a fund from your bank account, and you can arrange automatic transfers from a fund to your bank account to meet expenses. Most major fund companies offer

extensive record keeping services to help you track your transactions, provide tax information, and follow your funds' performance.

Disadvantages—As with any investment, mutual funds come with some disadvantages:

- **No guarantees**. Unlike bank deposits, mutual fund shares are not insured or guaranteed by the Federal Deposit Insurance Corporation (FDIC) or any other agency of the U.S. government. However the vast holding of the major mutual fund families serve as some degree of protection.
- **Fees.** A combination of sales commissions (except for no-load funds) and operating expenses need to be paid by the investor. These will reduce investment returns. Look for no-load funds. These require no commissions (which are one-time charges). Fund operating costs, although normally kept low, eat into the returns you receive as a shareholder. Compare the fees charged by different funds. You will be paying these annually.
- **Tax impact**. Whenever a mutual fund sells shares of stock, they are required to distribute the capital gains (if any) to all the owners of the fund. Those distributions are taxed and need to be reported on your annual personal income tax return. A fund that frequently buys and sells securities may add significantly to your tax bill via hefty capital gains distributions. This would be particular vexing if you have to pay capital gains taxes in a bad year when the value of the mutual fund goes down.

Although there are many pros and some cons associated with mutual funds, there is little doubt that the new investor should focus his investments primarily, if not entirely, through mutual funds. The more seasoned investor might opt for selecting individual stocks, utilizing a financial advisor, in addition to investing in mutual funds.

As you probably now recognize, it is critical to know how to invest your money in the myriad of choices available to you. Distributing your money amongst these choices is probably the most critical investment decisions you will make. The next chapter will describe in more detail how to allocate and distribute your investments in a manner that gives you the best opportunity to grow your wealth without taking excessive risk.

Chapter 10

Growing Your Nest Egg—Investing 101

Handling your money appropriately is essential to your lifelong financial health. It takes many years of investing to become truly knowledgeable about the process. But the path to riches can be both exciting and profitable. Although investing may seem like some mystical power, there is really no magic involved and anyone can, and should, learn about it. Remember, it is never too late to gain the knowledge and develop the necessary skills to lead to a savvy financial life.

Becoming an active investor leads you into a new and stimulating world with many different forces at work. Market cycles are changing along with economic, social, and political events. Emotional responses to events generally cause the markets to overreact while financial analysts and TV commentators are constantly trying to assign causes to every hiccup. Combining these factors, results in a dynamic and perplexing set of situations. The interpretation of financial situations can differ widely between various experts because the economic climate is so complex that nobody can possibly see the entire picture. It's often impossible to explain market activities until long after the dust has settled. Fortunately, day-to-day overreactions tend to work themselves out over time as prices adjust to fundamental business and economic realities.

The health of the economy is probably the most important factor affecting the stock market as well as your job. Meanwhile, inflation and the monetary system impact what goods and services will cost you, and the amount of interest you'll pay. Investing, especially in stocks, is an act of faith in the ability of market economies to grow over the long haul as it undeniably has in the past.

10.1 Critical Factors—The Dirty Four and Five Letter Words.

There are two dirty words that the investor needs to manage—**fear** and **greed**. Fear causes the investor to stay out of the stock market or invest very little. This makes him/her susceptible to the ravages of inflation. Greed on the other hand causes the investor to take excessive risk, which can lead to disastrous results.

Risk is the investor's other four-letter word. Everybody is risk-averse to some extent. But exaggerated fear keeps too many people from making appropriate investment choices. The fact is that stocks and bonds have been highly reliable for long-term investors for close to a century. As mentioned in the last chapter, the stock market has never lost money over any thirty-year period. However, there is no guarantee that it will not let you down in the future

The following table explores the historical returns and associated volatility for different sectors of the stock market from 1926-1993. Volatility is a measure of the swings in price (both up and down) of the investment. The table is arranged in the order of decreasing volatility.

Asset Category	% Annual Return	Volatility
Small Company Stocks	11.7 %	Highest
Large and Mid Sized Company Stocks	10.3 %	High
Corporate Bonds	5.6 %	Low
Government Bonds and T-Bills	5.0 %	Lower
Bank Interest	Approximately 2%	Lowest

The higher the volatility of the investment, and the greater the risk, the higher the return tends to be. However, with high volatility comes the risk of loss and some sleepless nights for those who worry about eating. Many investors, realizing they are not financially well prepared for retirement, choose to ignore the potential for loss and invest in a riskier portfolio in order to make up for lost time. Of course this can result in higher losses instead of higher returns.

Buying into the stock market when stocks are historically high, and everyone is optimistic, seems to increase your risk. It also sometimes results in an initial loss of money that could take 10 years just to break even. Those who say: "the market always goes up", are people who just have a short memory and ignore the bad times. Meanwhile those constantly adding more money to their nest egg actually take advantage of the down periods.

10.2 Guidelines for Successful Investing

There are many "experts" around who will tell you they have discovered the secret of successful investing. Some of these folks have made large profits over the years. However the average investor, struggling to meet his retirement objectives, is not in a position to take unnecessary risks. The approach presented below consists of tried and true methods of growing your nest egg without taking excessive risk.

Buy and Hold—The buy and hold strategy involves purchasing stocks or mutual funds for the long haul and trading them very infrequently. This is particularly easy to do if you buy and hold mutual funds and leave the trading to the trained account manager.

Much of the success of owning stock is determined by market conditions. A rising stock price can be attributed to either growth of the economy (or the particular sector) or to the performance of the company itself. The strength in the economy seems at times to override the quality of the company. A rising or falling stock market often seems to take the majority of stocks along with it. However, the growth of the company or industry sector is also extremely important since it determines whether the particular company stock outperforms the others.

It is extremely difficult for you to predict the future of the economy. If you listen to the financial experts argue about whether a recession is imminent or not, you will realize that they can't even agree on whether we're actually in a recession or not. So what chance do you have in knowing when to sell your shares of stock? Few can predict the ups and downs of the market well enough to make market-timing a consistent winning strategy. Even if you were smart (lucky?) enough to beat the odds, frequent buying and selling could increase your taxes and trading costs enough to wipe out much of the additional gains.

Many financial advisors disagree with the buy and hold philosophy. They feel that they know when to buy and when to sell. Most advisors will show you statistics backing up their claim. Remember that the advisors all do very well when the market rises. But, ask to see their performance when the market drops. That will separate the men from the boys.

Statistically, much of the historical market growth is sometimes correlated with one's being in the market on certain high-flying days. Market rallies often occur suddenly and frequently with no warning. If you happen to be out of the market during those few days, you could miss most or all of the gains for that year.

It would take a magician to predict the direction of the stock market. Your best bet is to be a buy-and-hold investor.

Know your Limit for Pain—Some people can be philosophical and shrug off big market swings. Others can't sleep at night because the value of their investments is dropping. If you are a chronic worrier, you should consider building a portfolio with a more conservative mix of assets and accept the reduced growth potential. Hopefully you have enough money saved that this approach does not prevent you from meeting your goals. Otherwise you'll need to compensate by saving more money or setting your retirement sights lower.

Low Pain—Investors who have substantial nest eggs and are way ahead of their savings goals need to decide whether to minimize their risk to just meet their objectives or take some additional risk in an effort to build more wealth. For example, if you can meet your retirement goals with 2% asset growth, just put the majority of your money in treasury bills, CDs, or money market funds and sleep like a baby. Or should you take some additional risk by building a portfolio with a high percentage of bonds and low percentage of stocks to further enhance your nest egg and perhaps having something more to leave your heirs. Is this greed? Or are you just being prudent?

High Pain—On the other hand, if you need 15% growth to reach your goals, you can expect a lot of sleepless nights with a portfolio aimed at this possibly unattainable goal. You would undoubtedly be better off setting your sights lower to begin with. Rather than taking excessive risk, which could result in excessive losses, you could decide to work an extra year or so before retiring or continue working part-time after retirement.

10.3 Asset Allocation and Diversification

A curiosity of the market is that different asset classes grow (or shrink) at different rates and sometimes move in opposite directions. Creation of a portfolio by combining assets that move in opposite directions from each other can reduce the portfolio's total risk to a level below that of any asset alone and thereby optimize your risk-return ratio.

The Three Most Important Factors—A wise man once said: "The three most important factors in a successful investment plan are to **diversify, diversify, and diversify**. And then diversify some more".

Asset allocation involves spreading your investments among the three fundamental asset classes: **stocks, bonds, and cash.** The degree that you do this depends on your goals, risk tolerance, and time horizon. Asset allocation partially protects against major upheavals in the stock market since other classes like bonds tend to go up in value as stocks go down and cash holds its value thereby temporizing stock market loss. You should note that there are a number of other asset classes such as real estate, gold, commodities, and collectibles that are outside the scope of this book.

Going to the next step—**diversification** within an asset class—reduces industry and company-specific risk. Together, they reduce portfolio volatility.

The investor must also **diversify within each of these asset classes** so that the unexpected failure of a single company or single industry will not have a major detrimental effect on his nest egg. When some company stocks aren't growing—or are falling in value—other investments may be growing and partially, or fully, compensate for the losses.

The stock market can be brutally unpredictable. Neither diversification nor asset allocation guarantees against investment losses. For example, consider the recent stock market meltdown of 2000-2001, when stocks in large companies plunged over 40%. If you'd had a portfolio consisting of 60% in stocks, 30% in bonds and 10% in cash, you'd have lost only half as much. If you were solely in large company stocks, it would have taken you 4 1/2 years just to break even.

Although it sometimes appears that the various sectors of the market are moving in lock step with each other, the reality is that the relative performance between sectors is always changing. The top-performing sector last year may be near the bottom next year and vise versa. Sometimes the top (or worse) performing sectors will keep their position for two or three years. But change is inevitable. By the time a small investor recognizes the best sector, the good times are often over. Meanwhile, the poor performing sector that the small investor sold to purchase the "hot" sector may be ready for a rebound. That being said, the investor finds himself out of phase and ends up buying high and selling low. This is termed "looking in the rear view mirror" for obvious reasons. In addition the investor would probably get down on himself for making the wrong decision so much of the time

Effective diversification involves more than simply owning a jumble of different investments. It means selecting a mix of securities that may not react the same to a given set of conditions: investments that carry a low "correlation" to one another. For instance, if you choose stocks of two companies that make the same product and serve the same market, chances are that they will move in tandem when conditions affecting their industry change. In this way owning both would be unlikely to lower risk in your portfolio. Alternatively, owning stocks of companies that operate in different segments of the economy may help improve your risk-adjusted returns.

The easiest way for investors to ensure portfolio diversification is to invest in mutual funds that offer a broad range of sector funds. If you choose to create your own portfolio you will want to consider investing in index funds that mirror an entire market sector i.e. S&P 500 Funds or NASDAQ 100 Funds. Mutual funds also offer index funds.

The following chart outlines different investment choices indicating their performance over a 70-year period, ending in the mid 1990s. The chart indicates the returns for the different choices and compares them to the consumer price index (CPI) which represents the "inflation hurdle" to be surmounted to truly increase your assets. You will note that many of the investment choices, like Treasury Bills and bonds, only modestly exceeded the CPI. Considering that these vehicles are frequently taxed (unless held in a 401(k) or IRA Account), there is little, if any, "real" growth associated with them. Hence it becomes apparent that some degree of risk is necessary to grow your assets beyond the rate of inflation.

Relative Return on Investment

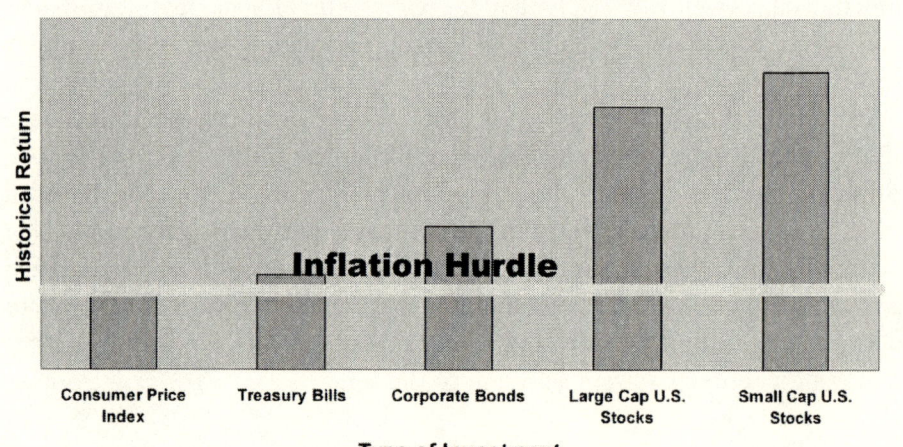

[Bar chart showing Historical Return for Consumer Price Index, Treasury Bills, Corporate Bonds, Large Cap U.S. Stocks, and Small Cap U.S. Stocks, with an "Inflation Hurdle" line. Type of Investment on x-axis.]

The 70 years covered by the chart have seen many anxious moments such as the final fall of Saigon, minor police actions (Haiti, and Grenada), and war with Iraq. We had nuclear confrontations and experienced the fall of the Berlin Wall. We had low inflation periods, very high inflation periods, boom times, and recessions. We had high interest rates and low interest rates. We had a strong dollar, and we now have a weak dollar. We had Democrats and Republicans in both Congress and the White House. Despite all this, the investor has done quite well during this period. But it doesn't mean he/she had nothing to worry about if so inclined. Depending on their particular personality, it took a combination of courage, faith, or a very laid-back attitude to stay fully invested over the years. Whatever it took, remaining fully invested in a diversified well-allocated portfolio was a key element of the investor's success.

Many believe that we will be hard pressed to maintain double digit gains in the coming years. It would be wise not to forecast those rates of return forever. A prudent person might reduce their expectations by 3-5 percent for planning purposes. If you get a better return, that would be great. If not, you haven't built a plan destined to disappoint due to overly optimistic estimates of future returns.

The years following this 70-year period have been particularly volatile with the emergence of large technology companies and the so-called "dot com" companies that have recently grown from their infancy. Unfortunately a number of these companies did not have appreciable profits to support their growth in stock price. As their stocks tanked, "newly wealthy" investors were saddled with major losses. The average return over the last 8 years have been well below the averages for the previous 70 years.

10.4   Personalizing Your Plan

Taking advantage of the gains possible in the equity market requires a willingness on the part of the investor to take calculated risks. The next diagram illustrates the relative risk associated with the various investment choices and the accompanying rewards. It should be no surprise that the greater the risk - the greater the reward.

Investment Risk vs Reward

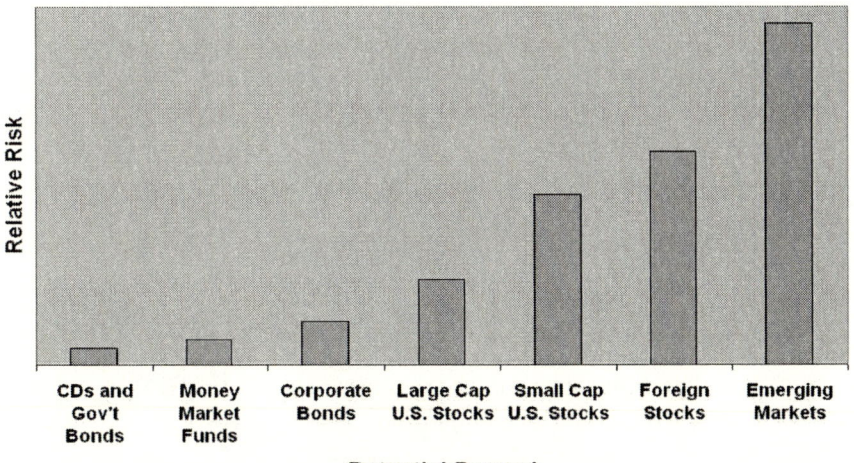

Relative Risk (y-axis) vs *Potential Reward* (x-axis)

Category	Relative Risk
CDs and Gov't Bonds	very low
Money Market Funds	low
Corporate Bonds	moderate-low
Large Cap U.S. Stocks	moderate
Small Cap U.S. Stocks	moderate-high
Foreign Stocks	high
Emerging Markets	very high

Your investment objective should be to obtain the largest possible rate of return without placing invested funds at more risk than is reasonable or bearable. The mathematics is complicated, but it can be shown that by allocating the investments among the various asset classes and diversifying within each class, the overall risk is reduced very substantially with only a small reduction in growth potential or reward.

Risk is frequently equated to volatility that can, in turn, be measured as a deviation from the mean or average price of the asset. The standard deviation (average deviation from the mean) is low if your returns have been relatively constant and high if they have bounced around a lot.

T. Rowe Price Investments has compiled a chart to depict how a truly diversified portfolio can help lower volatility with minimal impact on return. For example mid cap stocks, small cap stocks, and international stocks have greater volatility (standard deviation) than large cap U.S. stocks. Combine all of these investments and you will find that the volatility is significantly reduced (possibly lower than any of the components) with only a very slight impact in the overall historical return. So you should sleep a little better at night.

The chart below illustrates this relationship over the last 28 years. Note that the standard deviation of the diversified portfolio was lower than any of the components and the return was only modestly impacted.

Performance 1979-2007	Standard Deviation	Ave. Annual Returns
Different Types of Stocks		
Large Cap Stocks (S&P 500)	16.70	13.18 %
Mid/Small Cap Stocks (Russell 2500)	20.26	14.22 %
International Stocks (MSCI EAFE)	18.48	11.89 %
Diversified Portfolio		
60% Large Cap, 20% Mid/Small Cap, 20% Int'l	16.06	13.38 %

The chart is intended to illustrate the benefits of asset diversification on risk and return. You should note that there are a variety of ways to diversify a portfolio. The above portfolio is just an example to illustrate the principle and probably not appropriate for your specific situation.

Determining how to allocate your assets is a science in itself and will be described in more detail later in this chapter. But suffice it to say that you should base your particular allocation on a number of factors, including:

- Risk tolerance
- Years to retirement
- Living expenses
- Present savings

The above factors are used to determine the proper allocation for each couple. For example the above factors in your particular situation might call for a mix of 75 percent stocks, 15 percent bonds, and 10 percent cash. You might further break these allocations down as follows:

Stocks	Bonds	Cash
Income Stocks—10 %	Long Term Bonds—10 %	Checking Account—2 %
Growth Stocks—40 %	Short Term Bonds—5 %	Money Market Fund—8 %
Foreign Stocks—15 %		
Small Cap Stocks—10 %		
TOTAL STOCKS—75 %	TOTAL BONDS—15 %	TOTAL CASH—10 %

The asset class distribution used above is for illustration purposes only. A person close to retirement might want to have less than 75% allocated to stocks and more allocated to bonds while a person just starting out might want to have more than 75% allocated to stocks and less allocated to bonds. The general guideline is that younger investors can afford to be more aggressive because they have more time to ride out short-term drops in the market cycle. Older investors should have a more conservative plan, particularly as they get closer to retirement.

10.5 Investing in Stocks

As you probably now realize, you will need to invest a substantial portion of your assets in stocks in order to beat inflation and effectively grow your wealth. Individual stocks and mutual funds should be selected so as to develop a truly diversified portfolio. Hence you will need to understand the different options available in stock market investing. Stocks are categorized in many ways including size, age, growth potential, industry sector, location, and a host of other factors.

10.5.1 Company Size

Companies are often categorized by their size, i.e. large cap, mid cap, small cap, and even micro cap. Cap is short for capitalization and is calculated by multiplying the stock price by the total number of shares outstanding. Historically, large cap stocks have experienced slower growth and provided lower risk. Meanwhile small (and micro) caps have experienced higher growth but greater risk.

A common misconception is that the stock price alone is a measure of the size of a company. This is not true. One would need to consider the number of outstanding shares to determine the true value (market capitalization) of a company. The size, or capitalization, breakdown of different companies is usually categorized as follows:

Mega cap—This group is composed of companies that have a market capitalization of at least $200 billion. They are the largest publicly traded companies and include names such as Microsoft, Exxon, Wal-Mart, and General Electric. Not many companies can fit into this category, and those that do are typically the leaders of their industry.

Large cap—These companies have a market cap between $10 and $200 billion. Some of the well-known companies in this category are Yahoo, IBM and Citigroup. Typically, large-cap stocks are considered to be relatively stable and secure. Both mega and large cap stocks are often referred to as blue chip stocks.

Mid cap—This is a group of companies ranging in market capitalization from $2 billion to $10 billion and is considered to be more volatile than the large and mega-cap companies. Growth stocks represent a significant portion of the mid caps. Some of the companies might not be industry leaders, but they are well on their way to becoming one.

Small cap—These are typically new or relatively young companies, having a market value between $300 million and $2 billion. Although their track record won't be as strong as that of the mid to mega caps, small caps do present the possibility of greater capital appreciation—but at the expense of greater risk.

Micro cap—Sometimes called "penny" stocks, this category denotes market capitalizations between $50 million and $300 million. These companies offer great upward, as well as downward potential so they are not the safest investments. A great deal of research should be done before purchasing stock in these companies.

Nano cap—Companies having market caps below $50 million are called nano caps. These companies are the most risky. Nano caps do not typically trade on the major market exchanges like the N.Y. Stock Exchange, the American Stock Exchange, or the NASDAQ. They typically trade in the pink sheets or Over the Counter Market (OTCBB).

One should understand that the above ranges are not set in stone, but are known to fluctuate depending on how the stock market as a whole is performing. When the price of a stock drops significantly, the capitalization of a company will drop and may move the stock into another group. Understanding the market cap is not only important if you're investing directly in stocks. It is also useful for mutual fund investors, since many funds will list the 'average' or 'median' market capitalization of its holdings, letting investors know if the fund primarily invests in large-, mid- or small-cap stocks.

10.5.2 Phases of Company Development

Companies and industries go through natural phases as they develop and grow. The sequence of these phases starts with their emerging phase, followed by a growth phase, a mature phase, and then sometimes a declining phase. It is important for the investor to understand what phase the company is in before purchasing their stock since this sometimes indicates the potential for capital appreciation as well as risk.

Emerging Phase—Companies generally start out small in the early years of their development as small cap companies. A number of them will go out of business and not have a chance to develop into growth-oriented companies. For this reason, small cap companies tend to be relatively risky. It's common for the price a small cap stock to fluctuate 5% or more in a single trading day, something some investors simply cannot stomach. Small-cap stocks can trade on any exchange although a majority of them are found on the NASDAQ or the OTCBB because of more lenient listing requirements.

Because of their size, small caps have the ability to grow in ways that are simply impossible for larger companies. A large company doesn't have the same potential to double in size as a company with a smaller market cap. So, if you are looking for high capital appreciation and are willing to accept the risk of some loss, small caps are the way to go.

Small caps often have very little analyst coverage and so may be under reported. Hence there is a higher probability that small-cap stocks are improperly priced, offering an opportunity to profit (or overpay).

Growth Phase—Any firm whose business generates significant positive cash flow (or earnings) that increases at significantly faster rates than the overall economy is considered a growth company. They typically pay little to no dividends to stockholders, opting instead to plow most, or all, of it's profits back into expanding it's business. Earnings typically grow at an above-average rate relative to the rest of the stock market.

There are quite a number of growth companies found in the technology sector. A good example of a growth company is Google, which has grown revenues, cash flow, and earnings by leaps and bounds since its initial public offering. Growth companies such as Google are expected by many to increase profits markedly in the future, and thus the market bids up their share prices to higher valuations relative to their profits. This contrasts with mature companies whose stock is sold at a lower valuation due to their very stable earnings with little or no growth.

Mature Phase—An industry or company that has passed through both the emerging and the growth phases of their cycle is considered mature. Earnings and sales grow at a slower percentage in mature companies than in growth and emerging companies. A mature company may be near its peak valuation or just past it. While earnings may be stable, significant growth prospects are often few and far between. Mature industries are characterized by low increases in stock price and high dividends.

10.5.3 Value Investing

The objective of value investing is to find stocks that are under-priced. This may sound easy. But the reality is that in the age of the Internet and the resulting efficient flow of information, it is difficult to find under-priced stocks. The investment community considers many factors in evaluating whether to purchase, or sell, shares of stock. Therefore it is very difficult to find a stock price that does not truly represent the value of the company (intrinsic value) at that point in time. A stock may appear to be selling at a discount but there are often many reasons for the lower stock price.

The most widely used measuring tool for evaluating the stock in a company is the ratio of the price of a single share to the earnings attributed to a share, commonly termed "P/E ratio" The evaluation using this ratio not only considers present and past earnings but future earnings as well, generally resulting in two P/E ratios, present and future (forward). The investment community normally relies on the forward-looking P/E ratio that incorporates expected earnings in the calculation. There are many other measures that the prudent investor also considers including the ratio of the price to asset value, price to sales ratio, and price to cash flow ratio.

In the late '90s the price to sales ratio was considered the chosen method of evaluating technology companies since they had little if any profits. The technology industry was running at huge P/E ratios (sometimes even negative if they had no profits). These stocks were not appropriate for value investors due to their high valuations. The value investors, who seemed to be missing the boat in the late 90s, looked like geniuses in 2001 and 2002 when the technology bubble burst and the sector lost close to 90% of its value with many companies actually going bankrupt.

On the surface a relatively low P/E ratio appears to be a bargain but there are a number of factors that must also be considered. For instance some market sectors typically run at lower P/E ratio than others for a variety of reasons, not the least of which is their profit growth potential. Some company stocks are sold at a low P/E ratio because they do not have experienced management. In addition there could be a host of business issues that the trading market is aware of that is reflected in the lower P/E ratio. In this way the biggest challenge is deciding what a company's intrinsic value is and recognizing a good value.

10.5.4 Foreign Stocks and the Global Economy

International stocks can offer enhanced return potential and diversification when added to a U.S. stock portfolio. However, along with these benefits comes a higher level of risk. Through professional management and broad diversification, the inherent risks of international investing can be reduced but not eliminated.

The fastest growing companies today are located in what are known as the BRIC countries. These are Brazil, Russia, India, and China. India and China have the fastest growing economies of any large countries and so tend to provide the greatest potential rewards. But they also tend to be the most risky. What are some of the reasons for this high risk among foreign investments?

1. Analyzing foreign companies is a lot more difficult than analyzing U.S. companies since the reporting and record keeping requirements are in no way up to U.S. standards.
2. Many foreign companies rely on a large export market. In many cases they do not rely very heavily, at all, on their local market. This is because the market of choice is usually the United States consumer who has more money to spend than the people who reside in their own countries.
3. The currencies of some foreign countries are not very stable. In recent years, foreign stocks have been doing quite well expressed in U.S. dollars, since the US dollar has been very weak against many of the world's currencies. However, there have been too many incidents of foreign currencies virtually melting down due to internal political problems. This could leave your investment worthless. The riskiest investments are associated with the least politically and economically stable countries such as Russia and parts of Africa.
4. Political instability between countries can destroy certain businesses at times. For example what would you expect to happen if the U.S. and China stop, or severely limit, mutual trading with each other.

There are several ways to invest in the global economy. They include:

- Diversified international mutual funds
- Area-based specific (i.e. Asia, Japan, or China) mutual funds.
- Large multinational U.S. companies with world wide exposure

Overall, it should be obvious that selecting the foreign markets and specific foreign companies to invest in is not for the casual investor. It is not so easy for the professional investor either. However the potential rewards are so great that it is a good idea for every investor to have some foreign investments. Most financial professionals suggest that foreign stocks be limited to 10-20% of your investments. A conservative investor, or someone nearing retirement, might want to have even less exposure to the foreign market.

10.5.5 Stock Mutual Funds

Mutual funds are the fastest growing investment vehicles used by the American family. Back in 1980, only 2% of household financial assets were in mutual funds. Today more than 25% of their assets have been put into mutual funds.

There are two basic types of mutual funds. Open-end mutual funds are funds whose shares can be sold directly back to the mutual fund. Closed-end mutual funds are funds whose shares get traded on the stock exchange like stocks. The open-ended mutual fund's value is determined by the composite of the market values of all the stocks. A closed-end fund must be sold at the going market rate as determined by the price a purchaser is willing to pay. However the market price is generally very close to the composite market value anyway.

Stock mutual funds are an ideal way of diversifying. You can find single mutual funds that invest in the whole range of market sectors or mutual funds that are very narrow in their focus, investing in only a single sector i.e. technology stocks or bonds and anything in between. There are funds that specialize in almost any sector including: small caps, mid caps, value, growth, technology, foreign growth, foreign value, bonds, T-Bills, Japanese companies, European companies, Asian companies, etc. There are literally thousands of mutual funds from which to choose. A typical mutual fund can hold the stock of 50 or more different companies within the fund.

All mutual funds offer convenience to the investor as well. They do most of the record keeping and provide the information needed to file income taxes. In addition, many offer services such as check writing and easy transfer from one fund to another. Check writing, although somewhat limited, keeps your mutual fund money readily available for emergency situations. However this check writing privilege is not intended to serve as a checking account.

10.6 Investing in Bonds

Companies use three basic ways to raise money for expansion, acquisitions, and other uses. They can utilize their own profits, issue stock to raise money, or borrow money from investors. Corporations issue bonds as a way to borrow large sums of money. A bond is simply a loan that the investor makes to the issuer of the bond. The issuer could be a corporation, utility company, government agency, or some similar institution.

Owning bonds is very different from owning stock. If one owns stock in a company, he/she is a part owner of the company. A bondholder is not an owner but a creditor. Typically, the issuer of the bond promises to make regular interest (or dividend) payments and to repay the face amount (principal) of the bond when it comes due (reaches maturity).

Because bonds typically offer periodic payments of a fixed amount of interest, they're sometimes called "fixed income" investments. Maturity refers to the length of time before the par value is returned to the bondholder. It may be as short as a few months or as long as 40 years. At maturity, the bondholder receives the par value of the bond. However, if the investor wants to sell the bond earlier, he will be subject to the market conditions that set the value of the bond.

Bonds not only play a critical role in our economy but also have a place in a well-balanced portfolio. Overall returns from bonds, which include both dividends and appreciation in value, have historically been lower than from stocks. However, bonds are much safer investments since the Federal Government or large corporations back them. Bonds' safety and stability act as a counter to the fluctuations common to stocks. That's why most investors include bonds as well as stocks in their portfolio.

Governments and governmental agencies sell bonds to raise money for such things as mortgages, building roads, or performing other infrastructure projects for the public good. Because the U.S. Government backs them with its "full faith and credit", they are among the safest investments you can find. U.S. Treasury issues come in several maturities and denominations and frequently can be returned directly to the government before maturity. This reduces the interest rate risk very substantially. There is sometimes a penalty if the bond is not held for a minimum amount of time.

A bond's market value fluctuates due to changes in available interest rates or due to changes in the financial health of the bond's issuer. One of the most important things to know about investing in bonds is that bond prices and interest rates move in opposite directions. When overall interest rates rise, the value of a bond falls since an existing bond has a fixed rate. Conversely, when interest rates fall the value of an existing bond rises. For example if a bond is guaranteed to pay 5% interest and interest rates rise so that investors can now get 8% elsewhere, the value of the 5% bond is reduced. However the investor can always get full price (par value) at the bond's maturity. A bond scheduled to mature in 35 years will be more at risk to market fluctuations than a bond that is scheduled to mature in 5 years. Hence, long-term bonds normally pay a higher interest rate than short-term bonds.

A bond's credit rating reflects an independent rating agency's opinion of the issuer's ability to pay the interest on a bond and ultimately to repay the principal upon maturity. If those payments aren't made in full and on time, the issuer has defaulted on the bonds. Some issuers, notably the U.S. government, are financially stronger than others and are likely to have higher credit quality ratings. An issuer with a low credit rating will almost certainly pay a higher interest rate to compensate the purchaser for the higher risk.

Advantages of Owning Bonds—Some investors, especially retirees, hold bonds in their portfolios to get a steady stream of income. Bonds generally provide higher levels of income than most stocks or even money market funds. Bonds help to offset some of the volatility of stocks because bond and stock prices frequently move in opposite directions. Bonds tend to be less volatile. The regular interest payments that bonds generate can be reassuring to a retiree when stock prices are dropping.

Bond Mutual Funds are pooled sums of money invested in bonds. When a bond within the mutual fund reaches maturity, the proceeds are used to purchase different bonds for the portfolio. In this way, the bond mutual fund frequently cashes in bonds that mature and uses the money to purchase new bonds at their going interest rate. This tends to reduce the interest rate risk an investor would take if they bought only a few different bonds.

Managing Taxes—A bond investor should think about taxes. That's because the bulk of a bond's total return comes from interest, which the federal government, as well as the States (in some cases), typically tax as ordinary income. While bond prices fluctuate, capital gains (and losses), which are often taxed at lower rates, historically account for a very small part of a bond's long-term total return.

Investors can avoid paying taxes (temporarily) on bond interest income by holding their bonds in tax-deferred retirement accounts. Or they can invest in tax-free bonds (such as many municipal bonds) issued by State and local governments and agencies. Tax-free bonds generally have lower interest/dividend rates than fully taxable bonds. Each investor needs to evaluate his/her personal tax situation to determine if tax-free bonds are truly advantageous for the investor. Keep in mind that profit and dividends from taxable government bonds are often State tax exempt. Municipal tax-free bonds shouldn't be held in tax-deferred or tax-free accounts, such as a traditional IRA or a Roth IRA, since they are already exempt from income taxes.

10.7 Cash Investments

Cash investments don't simply refer to cash sitting in a bank account earning 2% interest. There are various types of very short-term debt securities that pay a moderate return and maintain the value of the investor's principal. They are a valuable part of any investor's holdings since they are used for ready funds and minimize loss in down markets. Although cash investments can't be expected to keep pace with inflation, they usually continue to grow, albeit at a very low rate, even in the worst of business climates.

The most common type of cash investments available to individual investors, are money market funds, bank savings accounts, short-term certificates of deposit (CDs), and U.S. Treasury bills. Only money market funds and savings accounts offer complete liquidity, which is the ability to easily withdraw cash almost immediately (within 24 hours) without penalty. The low returns on bank savings and checking accounts have led many investors, if they can accept the limited liquidity, to seek higher yields by investing some of their emergency money in CDs and short-term bonds which will mature in one to five years. Money market funds are a great compromise since they provide excellent liquidity with returns significantly higher than savings accounts although not usually as high as bond funds.

Money market funds are a type of mutual fund that invests in short-term (less than a year) debt securities of agencies of the U.S. Government, banks and corporations as well as U.S. Treasury Bills. Money market funds are very liquid, meaning you can take money out of them on short notice, usually at the end of the business day. There is no penalty for withdrawals from your money market fund, unlike Certificates of Deposit (CDs) that impose a significant fee for withdrawing your money. Additionally, you can write checks from your money market account (typically limited to three a month). The interest on a money market account is calculated daily, but only paid out at the end of the month unless you sell the fund, and then would be paid at that time.

Investments in money market mutual funds are not insured or guaranteed by the Federal Deposit Insurance Corporation. Both bank deposits and CDs (to some limits) are insured by the FDIC. Although a money market mutual fund seeks to preserve the value of your investment, it is theoretically possible to lose money by investing in these funds. It is however extremely unlikely because of the safe investments they typically hold.

10.8 Index Funds

The stock market has done so well over the years that many investors are happy just to be average. It has proved difficult to consistently beat average market performance. That is why there is a growing tendency for investors to invest in index funds. An index fund is one that mirrors individual sectors of the stock or bond market. They buy, in an appropriate ratio, all the stocks that meet a certain criteria like size or sector. Some examples of index funds are large-cap companies, blue-chip companies, micro-caps, small (Russell 200), bonds, and certain regions of the world i.e. Europe, Asia, or EAFE (International Europe, Asia, Australia, Far East). Perhaps the most popular is the S&P 500 index fund. This is a weighted average of the 500 largest corporations in America. These funds buy a cross section of the large company stocks in proportion to their capitalization and make no attempt to pick and choose.

Many people are not fond of index funds because they feel they miss out on specific high-flying investments. But studies indicate that, over time, index funds tend to outperform the majority of active portfolio managers. It is hard to accept that if index funds serve up average returns, that they have been able over the long run to beat most actively managed funds that invest in securities. But by eliminating the costs associated with researching stocks and keeping trading costs such as brokerage commissions low, they are quite competitive. After all, the computer does all the work, allocating your funds across the designated spectrum.

Index funds can also be purchased as ETFs (Exchange Traded Funds). These are funds that are traded on the stock market. Some examples are a NASDAQ index (QQQ) and an S&P 500 Index (Spiders). Unlike a mutual fund's end of day trading policy, ETFs trade throughout the day. For buy-and-hold investors a mutual fund trades often enough.

10.9 Balancing Your Funds

Once you understand the principle of partitioning your nest egg across the different asset classes and diversification within those asset classes, you are ready to develop a strategic plan. To the new investor this will seem like a daunting challenge. Keep in mind that there is help out there. The mutual fund families have worked it all out by developing investment vehicles that do all of the work for you. In other words there is now "one-stop shopping". These vehicles are termed "life cycle" funds or "target date" funds.

The goals of these funds are the following:

- Allocation across the types of investments
- Diversification across different sectors of the economy
- Maintaining a disciplined investment approach
- Providing the ease of monitoring a single fund instead of multiple investments
- Reallocating periodically to maintain targets

These target date funds allocate your investments among stocks, bonds, and money market securities in a manner appropriate for your targeted retirement date. Some also modify the allocation by a chosen degree of risk. These funds also diversify within the asset classes utilizing a mix of their own mutual funds. The allocation formulas have been developed in an effort to reduce your risk and still maintain significant earning potential. The asset allocation, in these funds, is more aggressive when you're younger and more conservative as you near retirement (the target date). The funds continue to grow, even after the target date, with the allocation becoming more conservative with time.

There are many such target date plans available on the market. They are similar in approach and intent but differ somewhat in their aggressiveness. For example one fund might suggest a portfolio containing 65% in stocks for a person nearing retirement while another may limit it to 50%. Neither should be considered right or wrong. The important thing is to realize is that as people approach retirement the percentage invested in stocks should be reduced (but not eliminated).

The holdings are periodically adjusted to maintain the targeted allocation. As one investment class grows (due to appreciation) relative to the other classes, that asset class will be partially sold. The funds will then be redistributed to maintain the targeted allocation. By the same token, if a class drops in value, additional shares will be purchased at the expense of a class that has grown in value. In this way the fund is generally selling high and buying low.

This targeted approach tends to generally out-perform the major indexes like the S&P 500 while taking less risk. This is all accomplished while making no forecasts, selecting no individual stocks, and not attempting to time the market. The investor won't need to watch the market 24 hours a day, or to trade stocks from your PDA from the golf course.

Target date funds are generally designed and selected based on your proximity to retirement. This typically means that a fund designed for a retiree in the near future will be much less aggressive than one designed for an individual who's 20 years away from retirement. The following charts illustrate this approach. The first circular graph, "2010 Retirement" has close to 50% combined U.S. and International stocks. While the following graph, "2030 Retirement" is much more aggressive containing roughly 75% stocks and includes far more international exposure than the 2010 Retirement portfolio. These charts are only intended to illustrate the principle. Check with the mutual fund families and compare their target date funds. You will find them similar in principle although the allocations will differ somewhat.

2010 Retirement

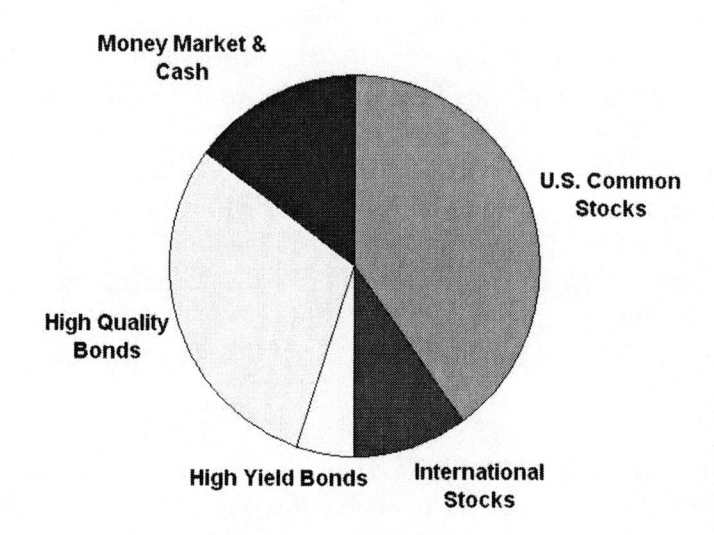

2030 Retirement

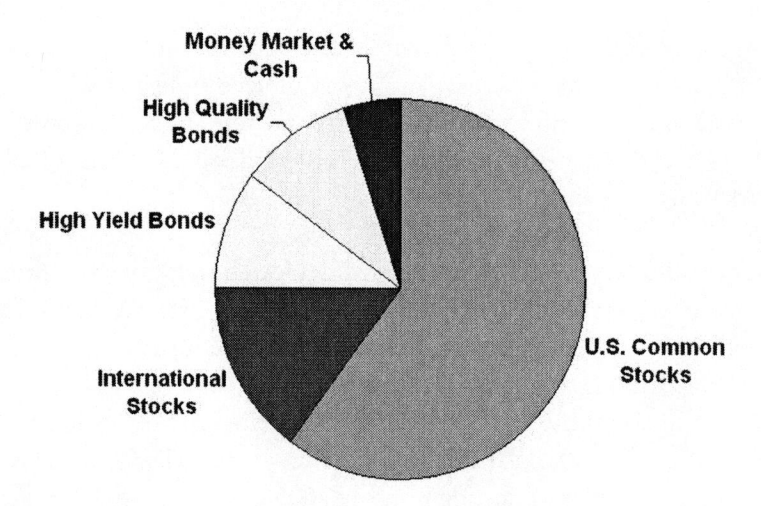

It should be noted that each sector indicated in the graph represents far more than a single investment and includes many different stocks, bonds, and treasuries. For example, the international stocks portion of the graph is composed of a few mutual funds representing different sectors of the international market that might include a European fund, an Asian Fund, an overall international fund, and/or some others. The U.S. stock portion of the graph could be composed of an S&P Index Fund, value and growth Mid Cap Funds, a Small Cap Fund, a Growth Fund, and/or a number of others as well. The bond portion of the portfolio could be dispersed among long term, short term, high quality and intermediate quality corporate and government bonds. The short-term holdings could be composed of treasury bills or very short-term bonds.

Typically each mutual fund company would compile this complex portfolio using their own individual mutual funds. Hence the target fund you might purchase from a fund family would likely contain in excess of 10 of their individual funds compiled in such a manner as to meet the overall declared strategy. Each individual fund would of course be professionally managed.

These Retirement Funds should not be considered a complete retirement solution. When planning for retirement, you should also think about factors such as emergency cash reserves, insurance, other asset holdings like real estate, collectibles, and the amount of equity in your home. Before investing in one of these funds, be sure to weigh several factors, such as your objectives, your time horizon, your risk tolerance, as well as your retirement needs.

Chapter 11

Early Retirement

The Declaration of Independence states that the "pursuit of happiness" is an inalienable right of every American. Unfortunately this is only true for those who can afford it. It's difficult for a wage earner to be happy much of the time since the pressures of the business world frequently conflict with those pleasures that he/she might wish to pursue. Every job can be unpleasant at times, to say nothing about being very stressful if not overwhelming. For this reason it is not surprising that the working person occasionally daydreams about having all the leisure he wants and not needing to work anymore. Hence retiring early is generally seen as something to strive for.

For many, early retirement has become the new American Dream. Unfortunately the increasing trend of early retirement is now reversing itself as more and more people recognize that they will not be financially prepared to retire as early as they had hoped. The fact that the younger worker must strive to be financially sound should come as no surprise. In fact the majority of this book is dedicated to providing insight into how to make financial independence possible.

Let's now look at some of the issues that, to a great extent, make early retirement so appealing.

11.1 The Window of Opportunity

As you age you go through a number of stages in life:

- In stage one, you are young and have all the energy in the world and time to utilize it. But you have limited financial resources to experience all that the world has to offer. Many of these experiences require energy more than money.
- In Stage two, you are starting a career and raising a family. You have neither extra time to engage in activities you enjoy nor extra money for the good things in life.
- In stage three, as your children approach independence you are tied down by your career and mounting bills. You have a need to save every available dollar for your children's college education and have little left over for your own retirement.
- In stage four, the children have completed their education and begun their own lives and are raising their own families. You are approaching retirement age. Hopefully by now you have diligently saved enough for your future.
- In stage five you retire and enjoy what's coined the "golden years". The first few years can be very expensive as you start to take advantage of your newfound freedom. You will likely travel extensively to take advantage of the freedom.
- In stage six, as you age further in the retirement years, your energy level and health start to slip. Your spending goes down as you lose the desire to travel and participate in activities like golf.
- In stage seven (if you ever even reach stage seven) you are old and infirm. Your spending needs go down unless you need to pay for assisted living or nursing home care.

As you can see, only in stage five, do you have the opportunity to enjoy the golden years. This is highlighted by the fact that you have the freedom and capability to pursue your wildest dreams (hopefully your spouse doesn't object). This period of time is your "window of opportunity," because you are still energetic (we expect), financially independent (we hope), and have reduced family responsibilities. It is a very special time because you hopefully still have the good health to reach out and enjoy your "pursuit of happiness". Unfortunately, this window never seems to stay open very long. One of the best reasons to seek early retirement is to stretch this window of opportunity. After all, you worked for it and you deserve it.

Widening the "window of opportunity" is especially attractive for you if you are an active retiree with an adventurous spirit. You may want to see the world by traveling to distant lands. After all there are so many places to see that, unless you can afford to travel around the world all at once, it will take at least 10 years just to hit the most popular places. The window is also important to the family-oriented retiree who likes to spend as much time enjoying the very active grandchildren as often as possible. It's easy to forget how much energy it takes to keep up with the little darlings, even for a short period of time, especially if you need to travel out of town to visit them.

Today most people tend to be reasonably healthy and energetic until reaching their early to mid 70s at which time both health and energy level deteriorate very rapidly. A healthy person that retires at 65 hopefully has 10 energetic years to enjoy. The same person retiring five years earlier, at 60, can hope for 15 active years until reaching their mid 70s. This increases the work-free window from 10 years to 15 years, a 50% increase (when compared to retiring at 65). Anyone lucky enough to be able to retire at the age of 55 will actually double the duration of this window of opportunity.

Do you feel energetic enough to keep working? Remember that a person retiring in their late 60s will in effect narrow the window appreciably, possibly reducing this window by 50%. The situation becomes more complex when you consider the difference in age between a husband and wife. Waiting for a younger spouse to retire (say at 65 years of age) will reduce the number of quality years they can spend together in retirement. For example if one spouse is 5 years older than the younger spouse, he (or she) will already be 70 years old when they are both retired together. This would reduce the quality time they can share by 50% and provides an added incentive for the younger spouse to retire early.

11.2   Advantages of Retiring Early

Retirees come in many shapes and sizes. But basically they can be broken into two groups—the business as usual group and the adventurous (mountain-climbing?) group.

Pursuing Passions—some retirees enjoy their day-to-day life so much that they have no desire to make any major changes in their life. They tend to be homebodies, having no desire to explore outside their local interests. They stick to their weekly routine and faithfully pursue their ongoing activities. They engage in hobbies like exercise, cooking, reading, gardening, writing, bike riding, swimming, taking a class, going to local events, and even doing volunteer work to feel worthwhile. These aging homebodies will eventually find it more difficult to take part in the activities and hobbies that they enjoy as the years creep up on them.

The more energetic wage slave might have a long list of things he/she would rather be doing if only they had the time. The list can include things like spending two hours every day getting buff at the gym, biking across country, leaning how to sky dive, playing golf three times a week, visiting out-of-town grandchildren, taking hunting trips, climbing mountains, taking fishing trips, and visiting far away places. Participation in any of these activities is rather limited during the working years when there is such little time to pursue these dreams. Even the annual 2-week vacation seems too short and rushed. The main reason people favor early retirement is to have more time to explore these passions.

Starting a New Career—Some people want to pursue a business of their own or they may have a career itch that they simply need to scratch. Consider individuals who worked for most of their life in a job (or profession) that stifled their creativity. Perhaps they want to become a teacher, open a restaurant, write a novel, paint for profit, raise orchids, care for animals at the ASPCA, or almost anything else. Basically they want to refocus their career to have more personal meaning. Sometimes that leads to working at the new career beyond 65 years of age just to satisfy that creative thirst.

Of course there's a big difference between retiring early to become a teacher and opening up your own florist shop. Starting a new career that only requires an investment of time can be exciting with little risk since you can always decide to fully retire whenever you choose. The person opening up a new business will generally need to put up a fair amount of money to start that business. In this case there are serious financial repercussions involved in walking away if you change your mind and decide that this business wasn't right for you after all. As a retiree you must carefully review your finances before putting them at risk this late in life. It would be prudent to confer with a financial planner before embarking on any change in career that requires a significant investment of capital.

Leave the Rat Race Behind—The second most prominent reason people give for retiring early is that they are just plain sick of living the rat race of the business world. Workers bringing home a paycheck are also bringing home the daily pressures that come with any job. They must be concerned about meeting schedules and producing a high-quality product in order to meet the expectations of their bosses. This places even more stress on the ageing workers who are expected to know more and be more productive. After 40 years in the rat race, many are tired of having to obey rules and keep an overbearing boss placated. Some are just plain exhausted after a lifetime of shift-work that often includes working nights and weekends.

Avoid or Prevent Deteriorating Health—Daily job pressure can be unpleasant. But far more important is the fact that stress has a significant impact on an individual's health. High blood pressure with resulting circulatory and heart ailments, emotional problems, diabetes and obesity are among the physical problems that could result from job pressure. The health impact can be especially severe for the 50 or 60 year-old worker in a management position where the expectations and pressure can be overwhelming. Most doctors believe that ailing health due to job-related stress increases with age. That being said, retiring early can actually be viewed as a lifesaver.

11.3   Disadvantages of Retiring Early

You've looked forward to the day of freedom for years. Now you're retired and you're not sure what to do. Why is this? Why don't many early retirees fulfill their dreams?

- Do they lose their drive?
- Are they unable to handle their newfound freedom?
- Do they just sleep in and watch television all day long figuring that freedom means relaxing on the couch?

Is this what you want after working for all those years?

Reduced Adjustment Period—The workplace fulfills a number of social needs for the worker. Yet the worker is seldom aware that he has benefited from the many social aspects of the work environment. The social factors, as explored in Chapter 3, include:

- Companionship and human interaction
- Structure or order from schedules and regular meetings
- Sense of identity and accomplishment

The early retiree may not have much preparation time if his (or his employer's) decision on early retirement is rather sudden. Nevertheless, the last thing on his mind would be fulfilling the social needs described above since they are usually not even recognized. After all there is no formal training in preparing psychologically for retirement.

The employee is ready to stop working and start enjoying his leisure. He concentrates on looking ahead to the last days of work, to feeling free at last. Then when the day comes, his senses are heightened as he leaves for home after his going away party with a skip in his stride and hope in his heart. Now as an official retiree, he soon finds that something is missing and he has no idea what it is. Perhaps the early retiree would be better prepared with more time to reflect on these needs.

Social Needs—Will your spouse and your friends still be working when you retire? Will you find yourself without a golfing partner? Will your spouse be unable to get away from work to enjoy your days with you and perhaps live out your dreams of traveling together? Will you feel friendless and have nothing to do? Being socially prepared for the many days, months, and years of retirement is, in many ways, just as important as financial independence. The early retiree is more vulnerable to these social shortfalls than a person who waits for full retirement and also may need to wait longer for his spouse or friends to retire as well.

Responsibilities—It is often a big surprise that retirement doesn't lift all responsibilities from a retiree's shoulders. They still have to care for family, parents, home, car, etc. Will their garage or basement paint itself? Will paying their taxes, monthly bills and chasing repairmen prove to be the true happiness that they thought retirement would bring? Maybe they expected too much and would have been better off waiting to retire.

Lack of Planning—For most people the depressing truth is that they aren't very organized, disciplined, or motivated enough to get the most enjoyment out of their retirement years. Often they're just plain lazy. They feel that putting together a plan for their retirement is too much like work, so they drop the task. Chapter 3 focused on the importance of a personalized retirement plan and also explained the concepts of activity planning. This Chapter will not dwell on this again, but will focus only on those issues uniquely relevant to early retirement. The reader is encouraged to go back and review Chapter 3 once more in an effort to understand the importance of planning for your retirement.

Financial Issues—Working for an extra year or two is a necessity for those who have not compiled enough of a nest egg to retire. It can also be desirable for those who have an adequate amount saved, since the last couple of years in a career usually correspond to the peak earning years. These last years of employment are frequently the ones where they can increase their savings as well as substantially increase retirement benefits via company pension, 401(k), IRA, and Social Security. Working for only one extra year, at your full-time job, frequently exceeds the earnings from working five or more years on a part-time basis in a job outside of your field.

The task of turning your savings into a reliable income stream that will support you for a long retirement is a challenge for all retirees. It's especially daunting for early retirees because, to begin with, they'll frequently be making larger withdrawals from their savings for a longer period of time, resulting in a significant drain on their nest egg. The early retiree will need to decide how to create this income stream in the interim before their pension(s) and Medicare benefits kick in. It is recommended that you carefully estimate your ongoing financial needs using the table presented in Chapter 4. This will help you to accumulate data that will give you a preliminary idea of your potential for success. Its best to then go see a financial planner who will utilize much more rigorous tools to help you decide how best to maintain your required income stream.

Pensions and other retirement packages generally reduce the benefits for early retirees. Even Social Security penalizes those who elect to retire earlier than the designated retirement date (typically 66 years of age). You can start collecting Social Security at age 62 but at a greatly reduced monthly premium. For two people retiring early this difference in monthly income can be very significant.

Perhaps the most prevalent financial issue facing the early retiree is the need for health insurance. If you are fortunate enough to work for an employer who offers health insurance for life, you're extremely lucky and should be congratulated. For the rest of us, health insurance has become such a major financial problem that it often is the deciding factor on whether to retire early.

11.4 Health Insurance

You've probably worked your whole career for a company that provided health insurance. In most cases your employer-provided health insurance will be discontinued when you retire. At 65 years of age, Medicare steps in and provides affordable health insurance coverage. Medicare-provided hospitalization insurance is actually free while the cost of medical insurance is reasonable and there are no pre-existing condition limitations. There are also a number of private Medicare supplements that are also reasonably priced and accept pre-existing conditions.

There is no doubt that everybody needs health insurance. Consider how you might fill the health insurance void if you're only 62 and your spouse is 60 years of age. In this case you'd be looking to find a way to provide health insurance for yourself for three years until you reach age 65 (when Medicare kicks in) and for five years for your spouse. Hopefully, neither of you is afflicted with pre-existing conditions or you'll quickly miss the lower health insurance costs you paid for coverage through your employer. You can expect that purchased health insurance for those under age 65 is going to cost more (often a lot more) than it did when you were employed. That's because most employers subsidize the cost of health insurance, frequently a large percentage of the cost. When you retire, you'll be responsible for the entire cost of the policy. (Note: those who served their country for 20 years in the military, or were police officers or firefighters are often able to retire in their early 40's with the government picking up the cost of lifetime health care. The rest of us have to make other arrangements.

Even if you've done everything else right in preparing for retirement, health insurance is one factor that could stop you in your tracks and prevent you from retiring early. More than 40 million people in the United States lack health insurance. You probably shouldn't retire early if it means joining them. Just remember that everybody needs health insurance since a severe medical problem requiring an extensive hospital stay can happen to anyone and without health insurance could quickly decimate most nest eggs.

What are Your Options?

COBRA—Under Federal law, when you leave a company you are allowed to continue your employer provided health benefits (medical and dental) for 18 months provided you pay the employer's cost of the coverage as well as your own. These are commonly referred to as COBRA benefits. COBRA stands for the Consolidated Omnibus Budget Reconciliation Act. Congress passed this law in 1985 to amend some rules regarding pensions and corporate health benefits. COBRA is a great way of continuing health insurance without concern about pre-existing conditions.

Your employer is permitted to charge you 102% of his total health premium cost. (The extra 2% covers administrative costs.) So if the coverage you had cost your employer $400 per month and you paid an additional $400 per month, you could extend that coverage for 18 months at a cost to you of $816 per month. By and large, it's a good deal considering the options. Other medical plans do not allow for pre-existing conditions and will either reject you or charge an exorbitant amount to take you on. Because of this, taking advantage of COBRA is a very effective way to continue your health benefits.

When your COBRA benefits expire? The Health Insurance Portability and Accountability Act of 1996 (commonly known as the Kennedy-Kasenbaum Bill) permits people who have exhausted their COBRA benefits to obtain individual health insurance policies for themselves and their dependents without restrictions on pre-existing conditions. This prevents the insurance companies from "cherry picking. The term "cherry picking" refers to the act whereby the insurance companies write coverage on the best risks (i.e., the healthiest people) and deny coverage to bad risks (i.e., people with pre-existing conditions.) Insurance companies are not anxious to insure people in their late 50s or early 60s. So continuing your existing plan could make good sense.

Several states have "guaranteed issue" laws that require insurers in the individual market to offer coverage regardless of a person's health. Many of these "guaranteed issue" state laws are actually broader than the requirements of the Kennedy-Kasenbaum Bill.

Purchase an HMO or Low Cost/Poor Coverage Health Insurance Policy—If you believe that your medical expenses will be minimal, this can be an effective strategy. However, if you're wrong, it can severely impact your nest egg in a hurry to say nothing about affecting your health. So don't take a chance. Now that you and your spouse are getting older the risk of significant medical bills goes way up. It can be frustrating to try to get an HMO to cover many expenses. HMOs tend to also limit access to certain medical professionals and diagnostic tests. In this way, you may be tempted to minimize your doctor visits and diagnostic tests to those that are absolutely essential, thereby compromising your health.

Be prepared to do your homework in researching any HMO you are considering. Ask the HMO representative specific questions about their policies and practices. Some of the issues of concern: Is your primary care physician in the HMO? How long will you have to wait for an appointment or diagnostic test? What is required to get approval for certain tests? Are there any other factors specifically related to your medical history? Make sure you have a clear picture before investing in your future health care. Chances are high that you or someone you love will need it sometime soon after retirement

Buy a High-Deductible Health Insurance Policy. When you purchase a high-deductible plan, you will be protected against major medical expenses. However you will need to pay for the ongoing aches, pains, and minor illnesses without help from insurance and these can be expensive. If you are considering this approach, you should review your medical history, associated office visits, and minor tests over the last 3 or 4 years. It is hard to extrapolate the costs to future years as you approach the age of 65 since your medical needs will increase as you age. Expensive blood tests, MRIs, CT Scans, mammograms, heart monitoring, colonoscopies, prostate exams, and other tests associated with ageing become more critical with each year as you age. The list grows every day.

Chapter 12

Outliving Your Money

There are many retirees who have such a large nest egg that they don't need to worry about outliving their money. Unfortunately, most of us aren't lucky enough to fall into this category. That is why the majority of retirees need to closely scrutinize and control how they spend their money. Retirees who must control their spending need to be careful that they don't fall into the following two groups:

- Those who are too conservative and don't enjoy their lives enough
- Those that are too free-spending (enjoy their lives too much) and run out of money too soon

Retirees who are too conservative deprive themselves of the lifestyle they worked so hard for, and deserve to enjoy to the fullest. Those who live "high off the hog" are putting themselves in danger of running out of money and being forced to seriously curtail their enjoyment of their later golden years. Will you be one of these?

You should analyze your situation carefully as you enter the retirement years. The worksheet in Chapter 4 can be used as a start to compile your past and expected future expenses as well as outlining your future expenses. Then sit down with a certified financial planner (not an investment advisor) who will run a rigorous spreadsheet to determine the probability of your being able to live the lifestyle you desire upon retirement. This spreadsheet is an excellent planning tool used to determine the percentage return you will need from your investments in order to provide the retirement income you desire and the associated risk you will need to take. Keep in mind that there are a number of unknowns in the projections that make the accuracy questionable. These unknowns include, but are not limited to, the health and life expectancy of both you and your spouse, the rate of inflation that will prevail over the next 20 or 30 years, the performance of your investments in that period, and the unexpected family emergencies that tend to sneak up on us. Nevertheless, running the spreadsheet will give you a good idea of what degree of caution should be exercised in your spending and investing in order to avoid running out of money prematurely.

There are a number of issues that you will need to understand as you approach retirement life.

12.1 Spending Early vs. Spending Later

Many retirees are so worried about outliving their nest egg that they unnecessarily skimp on life. The previous chapter pointed out that there is a narrow window where your health and energy level are adequate to enjoy life. Therefore your early retirement years could very well be the most expensive as you start traveling to distant lands and spending time visiting out of town relatives while you have the energy to do so.

In Chapter 3 you developed an activity plan, to follow to assure an enriched retirement. This plan likely included a number of hobbies and activities that require you to be healthy and energetic to get the most benefit. For example activities like tennis, travel, or bowling should be started early in your retirement program. There is less of a sense of urgency for more passive activities like reading, walking, golf, painting, writing a novel, etc. It is interesting to note that the more active pursuits tend to be more expensive than many of the passive ones. Some activities like travel can be downright expensive. Therefore, it makes sense that you would want to spend more money early in your retirement years while you can still enjoy it.

Hopefully you can participate in the more exciting activities early in your retirement and still keep within the guidelines that will be presented in this chapter without "breaking the bank". If not, you will need to make a decision on how much financial risk you want to take. Keep in mind that you can always make adjustments in some of your expenses to be able to offset these preferred activities without draining your nest egg.

12.2 Controlling Discretionary Spending

Discretionary expenses are costs that you can control. Minimizing selected discretionary expenses is a good way of having more money to spend on other activities without exceeding the recommended drawdown of your savings. The key is to make good healthy choices that allow you to prosper socially without significantly affecting your finances. Would you rather use your funds to play golf twice each week or be limited to playing golf once a month so that you can drink at the local pub regularly? Would you rather drive a very expensive car or take an annual trip to Europe? Would you rather eat out at a good restaurant once a week or eat out at a less expensive restaurant three times a week? These are choices you might need to make. Only you can decide what makes sense for you. We will present a number of examples of discretionary expenses so that you can evaluate which ones you truly feel are worthwhile for you.

Obviously insurance costs, medical expenses, mortgage payments, taxes, and repairs are items over which you have very little control. So what's left? Big-ticket expenses like travel, cars, and your out-of-pocket costs like restaurants, groceries, and shopping. This may be a good time to review chapters 5 and 6 again to make sure you get the full picture. Although these earlier chapters were aimed at reducing costs to save for those golden years, many of the same issues also apply to the retiree, but in a different way. Let's consider the following discretionary expenses that a retiree can indeed control.

- **Alcoholic beverages**—Limit the purchase of alcoholic beverages in restaurants and bars to only special occasions. Pushing alcoholic beverages are how these establishments make their profit. It's OK to have bottles of bourbon, vodka, gin, scotch or 6-packs at home and partake occasionally. Why not invite your fellow retirees a couple of times a week for home-made happy hours. You and your friends can share the cost by alternating homes for the happy hour.

Better yet, limiting alcoholic intake will make your wallet fatter and your stomach thinner—not to mention all the health benefits

- **Grocery shopping**—Shop at large low-cost supermarkets and consumer clubs. Purchase in bulk where appropriate. Try to take advantage of store sales-prices since you have the time to shop at multiple food stores if you choose. Just be careful not to spend more in gasoline than you are saving in food costs.

  Also limit the purchase of "special treats" which are generally bad for your health as well as being overpriced. Shop infrequently and never when you're hungry.

- **Restaurants**—Upscale restaurants can be an expensive proposition. Especially if you like to dine out often. There's no shame in eating at a family restaurant. Take advantage of early bird specials, restaurant coupons, and senior discounts. Limit the purchase of desserts, beverages, and especially alcoholic drinks. These tend to substantially increase the bill and tend to develop into unhealthy habits.

  Eating out should not be a daily ritual. An effective plan might be to eat dinner at inexpensive restaurants two or three times a week and limit eating out breakfast or lunch to only when you are away from home.

- **Entertainment**—Learn to take advantage of local outdoor events. Limit your visits to the live theater to special occasions like birthdays and anniversaries. Stay away from full price movie tickets—go to late afternoon or matinee shows that are less expensive, and never forget to take advantage of senior discounts. Don't purchase overpriced theater snacks instead use the money you save to help pay for dinner.

  Take advantage of the public library. Not only is this your opportunity to catch up on all the reading you never had time to do while working, but you can also attend book readings, browse through newspapers and magazines, rent recent DVDs for little or no cost, and attend book discussion groups. Read books for free and see recent movies for $1—what a deal.

If you live near a major city, you might make an inexpensive day of it by taking public transportation into the city and visiting the city park and going to the local museum. Ask your fellow retirees to join you and it's now a group social outing.

- **Purchasing the latest gadgets**—There is no limit on how much you can spend on the latest technical gadgets like I-phones, mp3 players, and BlackBerrys. Avoid purchasing things you really don't need. Your computer should last close to 4 years. Don't purchase a lap top computer unless you really need it. If you choose to buy a lap top computer, you may not need to replace your desktop computer. Do you really need a 60" TV in your 12' by 18' living room? Is high definition TV with expensive cable something you can't live without?

- **Gambling**—Going to the casino can be a memorable (unforgettable?) experience, especially if you drop a few hundred dollars at the tables. Casino managers make it so easy for you to frequent their establishments. They even sponsor bus service to the casino for virtually no cost. But avoid "taking advantage" of this. You will be left at the casino for a number of hours with nothing to do but lose money. The solution is to go infrequently, like every couple of months, and limit your losses for the evening to a small amount that you know you can afford. Consider this the cost of entertainment. Don't go with the expectation of winning. You'll probably leave disappointed.

There are many forms of gambling available today. You can buy lottery tickets, go to the horse or dog races, visit Jai Alai, go to off-track betting parlors, play poker with your friends . . . the list goes on and on. Many of these can prove quite entertaining. Just limit the amount you bet. A day at the races with your fellow retirees, where you only bet $2 on each race can be a low-cost entertaining afternoon or evening.

Be careful of Internet gambling. As a retiree, there will be plenty of free time to sit in front of your computer monitor and lose money. Avoid this like the plague. It can get very expensive in a hurry.

- **Buy a less expensive car**—You don't need a big gas guzzling SUV anymore. You don't even need a full size car. Buy an economical gas miser, and you'll save not only the lower purchase price of the car but on maintenance costs as well. In addition you'll find that the smaller car will last longer, thereby further adding to your savings.

- **Own one car instead of two**—Do you really still need two cars once you and your spouse have both retired? Sell, or at least avoid replacing, one of your cars and learn to live with a single car. It's not that difficult. Two people tooling around town in separate cars will only add to your costs. Have you seen gas prices lately? That should convince you that filling that second car just isn't worth it anymore.

- **Drive instead of fly**—The cost of travel can be very expensive. For some trips, driving is prohibitive, but for others it is not. If you decide to fly, your travel costs go up very quickly. Just remember, you need to pay for an airline ticket, find a way get to the airport, and then rent a car when you arrive. Flying is necessary when time is of the essence, but a retiree can usually afford to take the time to drive.

  Consider what you're missing out on if you choose not to fly. You are not stuck with an exact schedule and so don't have to rush to the airport. These days the airlines ask you to get to the airport 1½ hours before the flight. Then the flight is frequently delayed and you're just sitting around the airport with nothing to do. Have you ever been out of town and had your flight canceled? Now you know what stress is. How about arriving in the wee hours of the morning due to flight delays? Sure driving can be like work, but with your spouse beside you to share the driving there's so much less stress involved for the retiree.

- **Be less generous on gifts**—Your children and grandchildren need to understand that now that you're retired, you've removed the ATM machine from your front lawn. They will need to reduce their expectations of the financial help you can give them. You'll be surprised to find that if you buy them personal but inexpensive gifts, they will appreciate the less expensive gifts more than they ever appreciated the $200 check deposited in the bank for their birthdays.

- **Move out of that old house**—The maintenance on a large house can be very expensive, even if you do your own repairs. Add in the real estate taxes and utility costs and you'll likely find that apartment or condo living can leave you with less grief and more money. Home ownership also greatly complicates travel, especially if you plan to get away for the whole winter. You'll need to be concerned about snow removal, a flooded basement, and frozen or broken water lines. Just lock the door to the apartment or condo, have your mail transferred, and you're ready to go.

  The retiree needs to simplify his/her life. He should no longer be responsible for lawn care, home repairs, leaf raking, snow blowing, etc. Even if there is someone else doing the chores, the retiree is still responsible to ensure that they get done. And who needs the stress of chasing down a lawn care or snow removal service? Condo or apartment living eliminates most of these concerns. Plus, it's an excellent way for the retiree to remove the equity from his home. After all he may need it to live on.

- **Recreation**—Going to a ski resort in the winter and to the mountains or lake in the summer is certainly worth doing, provided you can afford it. However most retirees can't afford to do this very often if at all. But don't fret; there are many inexpensive, or even free, sources of recreation that can make your retirement days enjoyable.

  Save money by <u>not</u> joining the local health club. Instead try to arrange your own physical fitness program and incorporate some of your fellow retirees as well. Go biking or walking every other day along with some friends. You'll be amazed how the stimulating discussions will make the exercise enjoyable. You can do aerobics in front of your TV set with an inexpensive Jane Fonda video. Just buy an inexpensive set of weights or dumbbells for your bedroom and you and your spouse can stay fit for free and have fun doing it.

- **Volunteer**—Volunteer activities will keep you busy doing something useful. At the same time it'll keep you from running around spending a lot of money on various endeavors. Did you ever want to run for office, help deliver meals to seniors, work on a community beautification project, or teach a subject you're knowledgeable on? Well now you have the chance.

12.3 Living the Simple Life

As you can probably imagine, living simply is an excellent formula for making your retirement money last. The attitude that most have somehow adopted is that bigger (and more) is better. Larger cars, more food, a better wardrobe, and electronic everything seems to be a goal that many have strived for. In fact many people always seem to be striving for more in an effort to find fulfillment. This approach has taken a toll on the nation's psyche as well as on the earth itself.

Did you notice that the adults with the most toys were not necessarily the happiest people? Personal consumption does not seem to lead to satisfaction. Recent studies indicate that the choices we make are really not making us happier. We now know that once the basic needs are met, more possessions don't make people happier and may even add to their level of dissatisfaction. Once the novelty passes and the credit card bills come in, we find that the assumption that more and more acquisitions improve our lives is just not true. All the recent technological progress seems to have had no positive effect on satisfaction and may have actually reduced it. What most people don't realize is that simple living is also a good way of increasing personal satisfaction while enjoying their retirement years.

There are some people who seem to march to a different drummer and live a life of "voluntary simplicity". These people even take it to an art form. They tend to feel blessed with whatever they have and are not looking to expand their possessions and life experiences to live what most consider the "good life". Disciples of the voluntary simplicity principle typically feel that they already have enough to meet their wants as well as their needs and have no desire to have more. This might be a good way for a retiree to learn to live on less, by moving into smaller quarters, without feeling deprived. Proponents of voluntary simplicity don't understand the feeling people have for always wanting more. Some even carry voluntary simplicity to the extreme by growing much of their own food, doing most of their shopping at yard sales and resale shops, and constantly doing yard and landscape improvements around their own smaller home.

It is not suggested that you should evolve into a full-fledged disciple of "voluntary simplicity". But it's useful to think about how these people found happiness the next time you are confronted with a very expensive purchase.

12.4 Spending Down Your Nest Egg

The financial services industry and the media have gotten the word out that retirement is not affordable for many people reaching retirement age. But what should one do if they have not built-up $1,000,000 and are reaching retirement age? Some will keep working and others just tighten their belts and reduce their retirement spending to the bare essentials. Unfortunately, some people take this too far and are frightened to the point of believing they have to live like paupers to make their money last.

Skimping on activities during the retirement years deprives the retiree of the enrichment they've earned after toiling selflessly for so many years. Some of the more conservative retirees are afraid to draw down their nest egg at all and insist on only utilizing the interest and dividends in conjunction with their Social Security and pension (if any) to live on. The retiree needs to be aware that it's okay to tap the nest egg as long as it is done in a controlled manner. The best thing to do is to see a certified financial planner and have a personalized spending program put together for you. Remember that your money is there to be used. You should, however, be spending it conservatively to assure that it lasts for your lifetime.

Withdraw the appropriate amount. As mentioned earlier, the amount considered safe to withdraw annually is a function of a number of variables including your life expectancy (as well as your spouse's), the expected rate of inflation, the percentage you have allocated to stocks, and the expected stock market performance. The table below summarizes the percent withdrawal of your funds relative to life expectancy based on past historical data. Since there are so many variables, there is never a guarantee that the funds will last for your lifetime. But as a frame of reference, the 90% assurance and 98% assurance are considered good brackets. Less than 90% assurance is probably too risky for most folks, while 98% assurance might be too conservative. But the choice is yours.

Life Expectancy	10 Yrs	20 Yrs	30 Yrs	40 Yrs
98% Assurance	9.00%	5.32%	4.40%	4.12%
90% Assurance	9.78%	5.70%	4.71%	4.56%

Unfortunately, as outlined above, there are too many unknowns to make this table truly rigorous. But it does illustrate the difference in the spend-down of your nest egg for living expenses depending on your life expectancy. For example you could withdraw only a little over 4% of your assets for living expenses if you expect to need the funds for 30 years. If you only needed the funds to last 20 years, you could withdraw over 5% every year. If your horizon is only 10 years you could spend down your nest egg by more than 9% every year. But in reality, how many of us know how many years we will live?

Generally, it is felt that withdrawing between 4 and 5 percent of your assets initially, is a reasonable place to start. The withdrawal amount can be increased annually to compensate for the inflation rate. A good approach would be to use your Social Security, pensions (if any), and any other income to live on and then withdraw about 4-5 % of your money to provide any additional income needed. You should try to control your spending to match this income level. Note that the "acceptable" withdrawal amount should include any interest and dividends on your investments that are paid directly to you.

You needn't be a slave to the 4% rule that you will undoubtedly read much about. You could take that extra vacation or treat yourself to other splurges in the early years of retirement when you are more energetic and then pare back your spending in later years to compensate. But, you've got to follow through on this in the later years. Don't withdraw 5 or 6% for the first 10 years or you will be in real trouble down the road. Remember that you could run out of money before you run out of time.

Pay Attention to Taxes. Retirement is a good time to reevaluate how your investments are allocated among your taxable and tax-deferred accounts. You may be surprised to find that the investment strategies that worked well while you were saving for retirement could work against you when you start withdrawing your money. For example many people tend to hold most of their long-term-growth investments in their 401(k)s and IRAs and keep their "safe money" in taxable CDs and money-market accounts. That's fine while you're accumulating assets, but once you retire you may be better off flip-flopping the approach for tax purposes.

You are required to start withdrawing tax-deferred money from your IRA and 401(k) once you reach 70 1/2 years of age. Until that age, you should primarily withdraw your living expenses out of taxable accounts so as to minimize the total taxes paid and allow your IRAs and other tax-deferred accounts to compound for as long as possible. Once the taxable accounts are depleted, you then start withdrawing from your tax-free retirement accounts. But there are exceptions. Sometimes it pays to split your retirement withdrawals between your taxable and tax-deferred accounts now to prevent a huge tax bill later.

There's a big difference between the way investments are taxed inside a retirement account and outside of one. When you hold an asset for more than one year, and then sell it at a profit, you pay long-term capital-gains taxes at a maximum rate of 15% if the asset is held in a taxable account. If that same asset is held in a tax-deferred retirement account, there is no tax consequence when you sell it. But when you withdraw the money from the account to use for expenses, all of it is taxed—not just your profit—at your ordinary income-tax rate, which could be as high as 35%. The 20-point spread between the top ordinary income-tax rate and the long-term-capital gains rate can make a significant difference in your tax bill.

Tax rates can fluctuate from year to year for a retiree who has significant stock holdings. Even after retirement you may still be in a high bracket. Hence it is possible that it may pay to withdraw from a tax-deferred plan in a year with very high medical expenses, high stock losses, or other high tax deductions. In these cases you may want to take more than the minimum required withdrawal out of your traditional IRA or 401(k) and pay the tax on the withdrawal. It can get very complex; so make sure to stay in touch with your tax accountant.

Chapter 13

Myths and Realities

The previous chapters have provided the insight you will need to prepare yourself for retirement as well as managing your finances after retirement. We have focused on a number of issues ranging from the challenges of being financially, socially, and emotionally ready for retirement to the basics on how to be a successful investor. This book has addressed, in detail, how you can accumulate enough wealth to be able to adequately support yourself in a retirement life-style that you have earned after so many working years.

The financial management approach suggested in this book is intended to get you started and place you on the life-long learning curve to improve your financial well being. As a lifetime investor, I have been on this learning curve for close to 40 years and learned the meaning of risk and reward. We need to remember that taking substantial risk is not an acceptable solution since striving for great gains can result in significant losses to our retirement nest egg.

This chapter will focus on some of the myths and tales that we hear so often and compare them to the realities of successful retirement planning. Although there is nothing new presented in this chapter, it's a great way of pulling most of the principles together in your mind.

Myth No. 1—All is Lost if You Don't Have a Pension

It appears that a pension is necessary for an individual to reach financial independence. That means that a person lacking a good pension plan is doomed to work until they're 85 years old.

REALITY: Definitely not true!! There are many other ways to provide for a good retirement.

There is no doubt that baby boomers are less likely to have pensions than did their parents. More and more companies are dropping or freezing their traditional pension plans in an effort to cut the cost of providing worker benefits. You can no longer expect a pension that guarantees a generous monthly income for the rest of your life. In 2005 only one in 10 private-sector employees were still covered by pension plans. Even as you are reading this, the number of people covered by pensions is quickly dropping. If you have a good pension plan, you are one of the lucky ones. The size of the pension (for those who still have pensions) depends in large part on how long you stay with your employer. So if you switch jobs a number of times during your career, as most people do, you'll end up losing a large percentage of your benefits.

The defined-benefit pension is being replaced with company sponsored 401(k) plans, which allow you to have a flexible, 21st-century, career and still have a way to put away enough money to fund a comfortable retirement. The 401(k) is a portable account that the worker can always take with him/her upon changing employers. Your 401(k), coupled with your own personal IRA, needs to generate enough income to replace the monthly pension checks that you would not get. But it is up to you, the worker, to exhibit discipline and good judgment to grow these accounts.

Unfortunately, workers today are not well prepared to manage their own financial future. They did not have good role models since there was no real need for their parents to learn to do this since they had pensions and shorter life expectancies. You will need to get educated in a hurry. But there is plenty of help out there.

Myth No. 2—Don't Count on Social Security

Politicians are always reminding us that Social Security will soon be operating at a deficit. Vote for them and they will fix the system. They tell us that Social Security is in big trouble if the other party wins. The implication is that you won't get Social Security benefits in your old age unless that politician is elected to office.

REALITY: Don't believe them. Sure, the headlines are alarming but Social Security isn't going the way of the Dodo Bird or the BetaMax any time soon. The system can and will likely be fixed when it needs to be.

In just 10 years the government payout for Social Security benefits will exceed the amount that workers pay into the system. And in about 30 years, the Social Security trust fund reserves could run out, unless Washington gets around to addressing the problem. But that doesn't mean that Social Security will go out of business and disappear. The government can't allow that to happen for political reasons. Just listen to all the politicians running for office claiming that they have a plan to save Social Security. Obviously, they recognize the strong voting block that retirees, and near retirees, represent and wish to play into their good favor.

You should keep in mind that enough money would continue to flow into the Social Security system from payroll taxes to fund around 75% of the presently scheduled benefits until 2081. And with a few reforms, Social Security could continue to pay full benefits indefinitely. Fixing Social Security is relatively simple compared with the other spending issues the government faces, such as Medicare and Medicaid. There are a number of corrections being considered to fix Social Security. Most will be palatable to the public. For example just raising the payroll tax by approximately one percentage point for both employers and employees would allow the government to fund full benefits for the next 75 years. Other possible changes include increasing the age for full benefits slightly, increasing the tax able amount of Social Security payments, or just modifying the cost of living adjustment. A combination of these changes will be able to finance the projected shortfall indefinitely.

It is not clear what fix the government will finally pick. Retirees will likely be impacted by some of the changes but not as substantially as some may imply. So don't believe every fairy tale you hear. It's a good bet that you can count on receiving something fairly close to what retirees collect today from Social Security.

Myth No. 3—It Takes a Big Salary to Develop a Big Nest Egg

People believe that without a high salary, there is no opportunity to save for retirement. They feel that all their expenses are warranted and therefore there is no room for improvement. Since they can barely make ends meet now, how can they have enough left over at the end of the month to save? How can anyone hope to build up a significant nest egg when credit card balances are increasing monthly?

REALITY: If you still believe this myth, you need to go back and look through the book again. Most people earn enough to have something left over to save if only they would learn to bypass a few simple pleasures. It doesn't seem like it would make much difference in their retirement. But, over time, it sure can!

Anyone can spend less than they do today. Keep in mind that there are many families who manage to get by with much less income than you have. So don't think that you have no room to increase (or start) savings. There is so much waste in all of our lives that all you need to do is develop a better understanding about the necessity of saving and have the discipline to go out and do it.

There is a general lack of understanding about managing money. Very few are formally trained in the proper handling of personal expenses and it's not knowledge that you can easily pick up on the streets. Discerning luxuries and frivolous spending from necessities is not as obvious as you might think. The key is to reduce your spending to balance your checkbook and pay down your debt. Once you've eliminated credit card debt you can then start saving in earnest. As Chapters 5 and 6 demonstrate, everybody has significant opportunity to reduce wasteful spending. With planning, discipline, and a little ingenuity most people can build quite a substantial nest egg.

It's also important to realize that there is another side of the equation and that is to put your money to work for you. Take full advantage of tax-deferred money that will grow faster for you once you invest the money appropriately. There are plenty of resources available to help you invest wisely and make you look like a genius in the long run. But you must start now.

Myth No. 4—$1 Million Dollars in Savings is Necessary to Retire

At the rate most people are going, chances are they'll be 140 years old when they get to that point. So they expect to work until they die.

REALITY: The most prominent reason why people neglect to start their retirement savings program is because it seems so hopeless. Too many people seem to lack the initiative and creativity necessary to change their lives. But any of them can change if they really want to.

Some people will tell you that you need a million dollars in your retirement portfolio in order to retire. That lofty goal may be true in some cases but not in most. Of course it depends on your spending habits. For example, if you earn six figures, spend most of it every year, and have no intention of living on an austere budget when you stop working, you may actually need far more than $1 Million. The couple that spends over $100,000 per year on their living expenses could go through $1 Million pretty quickly if they keep spending at that rate once they stop working. Meanwhile a couple living on $50,000 per year can probably live forever on the same $1,000,000. How is this possible? Well, for starters a couple might receive close to $30,000/year in Social Security alone. This would mean they would need another $20,000 to cover expenses. This is only 2 % of their million dollars withdrawn each year. At that rate their million dollars nest egg may indeed last forever.

So how much of a nest egg does this couple living on $50,000 per year really need? Let's do the simple math. Using a conservative guideline of withdrawing 4% of the nest egg for the additional $20,000 needed each year, they would only need to have accumulated a nest egg of $500,000 prior to retirement. Drawing down their nest egg by a less conservative 5% each year would suggest a savings of $400,000 would suffice and could be reduced further if they were more thrifty. That's a far cry from $1,000,000

Obviously, the numbers will be different for each retiree. With a pension, part-time work, or more modest expectations, you can get by with significantly less than the example described above. So there is a balancing act you need to perform between how much you tighten your belt in order to save during your working years and how well you want to live in retirement. You can't have your cake and eat it too.

So how much do you need to have saved? Suffice it to say that there is no set "magic" number. It depends so much on your particular situation and your flexibility. The only number that really counts is the number you personally arrive at based upon your goals and resources. So start figuring. Allow a financial planner to use a retirement calculator to find out whether you're on track and how much you will need to adjust your standard of living (now and in retirement).

Myth No. 5—It's OK to Wait Until Tomorrow to Start Saving

People frequently wait to start saving since they feel that there is no "extra" money available. Then they invest in a portfolio that potentially yields a higher return to make up for lost time. Looking back at historical returns suggests that they can make up for lost time.

REALITY: Does this sound like you? If so, be careful. This kind of blind optimism can hurt you big time. Although it's true that the stock market has been very generous to investors in recent years, there is no assurance that past performance will repeat itself in the coming years. Many experts believe that the stock market will not be able to sustain its recent performance. They recommend that you not expect the high returns of recent years, upon retirement. Certainly a person approaching retirement should not take undo risk.

How do we describe a financially prepared retiree? This individual has little if any debts, has his assets properly allocated and can sit back and enjoys retirement. The properly prepared person has all the income needed from Social Security, pensions, bonds, T-bills, and money-market funds and withdraws no more than 4 % from his nest egg. He has one major advantage over the stock market amateur, and the neophyte trader—**HE DOESN'T TAKE UNNECESSARY RISK**. The well-prepared investor does not face the undue pressure of playing catch-up and "make a lot of money" in the market. This retiree relaxes by the pool with his spouse while his money is working for him.

The financially prepared investor can always focus on value. By rebalancing his portfolio, he ends up buying bonds when they are cheap and bond yields are irresistibly high. When stocks are selling at bargain prices he is buying stocks. In other words, he puts his money where the best value is. If no outstanding values are available, he will just wait. One can afford to wait and be patient when adequately prepared. Life is good.

Compare the financially prepared retiree with the person who starts late and so needs high returns (perhaps a 10-12 % return) every year to reach his goal. First of all, it will be very difficult to sustain a rate this high. Secondly, what does he do when the market turns down, as we know it will from time to time? He is now tempted to take even more risk than before and certainly more than he should as he approaches retirement. And you can just guess where this will lead.

Myth No. 6—Once You Reach 50 Years of Age, It's Too Late to Start Saving

For a 50-year old with only a small 401(k) account with under $50,000, the situation is hopeless. So why start depriving yourself now.

REALITY: These are famous last words from a true defeatist. It's really never too late to benefit from building your nest egg. All the articles state that you should start saving early in your career. Obviously, it would have been better to start saving earlier. But the truth of the matter is that most people don't. Although you can't turn back the clock, there's hope for all you late starters (even those over the age of 50). A few years of serious saving can make a huge difference in the quality of your retirement years.

The first thing you need to do is face up to the hard, cold, numbers. Review what you have saved to date (if anything) and determine how much additional money you'll need to save to compile enough for a decent retirement lifestyle. This exercise could very well prove to be depressing. But you need to go through it anyway. A financial planner can lend a helping hand in advising you how to save more and encouraging you by pointing out that your situation is far from hopeless.

From this point forward, you'll need to become very frugal and sock away as much as possible for the few working years you've got left. A working couple in their 50's without small children at home can save a lot of money from their salaries if they put their minds to it. You might be surprised at how quickly your efforts will show results. Taking full advantage of your 401(k) and IRA (including catch-up contributions for those over age 50) along with living as simply as you can for 10 or 15 years can allow you to accumulate hundreds of thousands of dollars before you know it.

This is not the time to procrastinate any further. Just get started now. You can't afford to waste any more time.

Myth No. 7—You Can Handle Debt

There are those who live with debt all their lives. Since they somehow find a way to eventually pay it off, they find no reason to deprive themselves of the things they want just to save for retirement.

REALITY: No. You should eliminate debt, not extend it. It is unbelievably expensive in the long run.

Most people suffer from overconfidence—but Americans more than anyone it seems. People tend to feel overly optimistic about their ability to pay back debt. Incredible though it may be, companies have layoffs, cars and homes do sometimes need repairs, teeth need major dental work, and surgeries may be required that insurance doesn't completely cover. Everyone needs an emergency fund for the big expenses that come, especially those unexpected. Borrowing should be left to your home mortgage and very little else. After all without the home mortgage, you would still be living in an apartment. The historically low mortgage rates are a fraction of your credit card rates.

The most readily available loans are the credit cards in your wallet. The credit card companies love for you to pay only the minimum each month. They then hit you with exhorbitant interest rates and penalties if you're even a few hours late. A person serious about preparing for retirement shouldn't carry over a credit card payment from month to month. Better yet, they should pay cash so that they better control their expenses. Most people are shocked to see the size of their monthly credit card bill. Their first instinct is that it must be a mistake. Look at the monthly bill closely and ask yourself if you would have made the same purchases if you were paying cash.

People need to be aware of the terms of any loans they make, including mortgage loans. Borrowers needs to be sure that they can afford the payments associated with their loans. Recent predatory loan practices have resulted in a number of families purchasing homes they could not afford. They were given lower loan rates initially, to make the homes appear affordable, and then a number of months later the rate increase makes their payments unaffordable. In many cases the homes weren't even affordable at the initially lower interest rates. This created the so-called "sub-prime mess" that has managed to impact the entire financial system. The message is: Buyer Beware!!!

Myth No. 8—Debt is Normal

Some people feel that borrowing is a path to financial freedom. They figure that if they don't pay down all their debts they will have more money to invest and can make greater returns. Borrow to financial independence. Now they may think they are on their way—but to where?

REALITY: Debt is just another four-letter word when you're saving for retirement. Borrowed money is expensive—plain and simple. Without taking unacceptable risk, it is close to impossible to make returns on investments high enough to meet the cost of borrowing. A credit card charges over 20% on the unpaid balance (loan shark rates). Try to get this return on your investments. Your car loan will be in the 10% range. Even that return will be hard to match. Hopefully long before the time you've retired you will have shed all your credit card debt. Now the questions you need to address are whether you should have a mortgage on your home(s) and car loans.

You should try to pay down all these debts by the time you retire. Start with your credit card loans first and continue to eliminate all debt to the point where your home mortgage becomes the last one to be paid off. A number of people feel that some of the lower advertised car loans are justified for a retiree. But don't be fooled. On closer examination you'll find that the special low interest car loans are in lieu of a rebate deal that would save you a significant amount of the cost of the auto.

Your mortgage is another story. You are likely to get higher returns in the stock market than you are paying for your mortgage. Besides your mortgage is tax deductible. It is not always a good idea to pay down your mortgage too soon, especially early in your career where your investments are fairly aggressive and your return will tend to be high. But as you reach retirement age, keep in mind that you should have less aggressive investments and be in a lower tax bracket and so it is probably advisable to pay down your mortgage.

Sometimes there is enough tax advantage associated with a mortgage to justify the higher interest rate. But that is rare and the evaluation can be tricky. To be sure you make the appropriate decision, discuss these issues with your accountant and financial planner.

Myth No. 9—You Owe it to Yourself

Every hard worker deserves that cup of coffee and piece of pie so you should go ahead and have it. After all, it will make you feel good. How about another slice for good measure? You should also buy the new expensive car that you would love to have. You deserve it.

REALITY: You think you are rewarding yourself, but you are actually penalizing yourself. Obesity from eating too much and the overriding thirst for materialistic possessions is destroying us. We now need larger homes just to hold all our things. The end result is a house and garage full of stuff and no money in the bank. Why do we do this to ourselves? Probably because we feel that we work so hard that we're entitled. For crying out loud, have some discipline.

Our calorie intake is too high and yet we're sometimes actually undernourished. Just like eating food for no good reason other than the fact that it is set in front of us, people buy needless things just because they see them. Shoppers buy sale items when they don't need them because they believe the word "sale" means they're saving money. But all of this stuff just takes up space, takes years to use up, or it just goes to waste.

Why buy an economy car when you can get a loan for twice as much and ride around in style? Over-buying is a trap the consumers easily fall into. After all, the stores and credit card companies depend on you to spend beyond your means. Often when making big purchases, the price seems so overwhelmingly high that even smaller add-ons or upgrades start looking reasonable in comparison. One rationalization could include, "Well I'm already borrowing $10,000 for this car, so what's another $3,000?" What you're doing is pairing the smaller purchase with the bigger purchase and all of a sudden the smaller purchase doesn't look so bad. Marketers are aware of this, so they add on lots of small extras that have huge margins (like warranties for instance) to greatly increase their profit.

Envy colors our perceptions. Expenditures we decide are reasonable may be based on what we view others purchasing around us. But because income disparities are so incredibly wide, what we view around us can easily be beyond our means. This is sometimes called "keeping up with the Joneses". Similarly many of us are trying to emulate the upper-middle-class families that we see on TV. Remember, living like the rich can make you poor in the long run.

Myth No. 10—No Price is Too Great for Your Kids' College Education

When you have children, you want only the best for them. So, college needs are more pressing than your far more distant retirement. Therefore, funding a college education is a family's top priority, ahead of retirement savings and the purchase of a house.

REALITY: Education is extremely important but don't let college tuition derail your other plans. You need to understand that "there is always more than one way to skin a cat". You can get your children educated without giving up your other dreams. As a mater of fact you can accomplish most of your goals if you just stay focused and dedicate yourself to making them happen.

There are very fine State colleges that provide excellent education at a fraction of the cost of private institutions. Most colleges provide student loans as well as grants so that qualified students can still attend the college regardless of the parents' means. There is no reason that the student can't shoulder a good portion of the financial load by holding down a part-time job and also taking out a student loan to be paid back after graduation.

Universities often provide loans and grants based on the student's high school performance. So a good first step is to make sure your child keeps up their high school grades and extra curricular activities. A part-time job will do wonders for preparing your child by giving him an appreciation for the value of a dollar as well as the responsibility needed later on when the student loan has to be paid off.

Don't assume you have to pay the full tuition or cover the debts that your child builds up while in college. Paying 100% of university expenses is a sure-fire way to ruin your retirement. It can drain enough of your savings to put you in a financial hole that you'll never dig out of. A reasonable goal, for most families, is to tap your savings for no more than a third of the costs (if you can afford it) and add some from your ongoing income. Then have your child make up the rest through financial aid, loans, and a campus job.

Don't let college tuition put a major burden on you and lead you to pass up your biggest and best weapon—the power of compounding your wealth over time. Tens of thousands of dollars invested and allowed to compound for 20 or more years can build up to hundreds of thousands of dollars when you're ready to retire. Just remember there is no retirement scholarship for you when you reach age 65.

Myth No. 11—When Changing Jobs I Should Cash Out My 401(k)

Changing jobs makes 401(k) money available to you. The money can be used to purchase a car or other things for the family or to take that vacation before starting the new job. After all, it may be a whole year before you are eligible for another vacation.

REALITY: This is a big mistake. You are missing out on a golden opportunity to build your nest egg by pulling the money out of your 401(k). You will need to let this money continue to grow. In addition you will have to pay taxes on the full amount of the withdrawal.

Typically, employees can expect to have a number of jobs during their careers. Most employers will offer the opportunity to enroll in their 401(k) plan. Some will even enroll you automatically. Unless you've been hiding under a rock instead of reading this book, you probably realize that the 401(k) is the best financial move you can make for yourself. But, when you change employers, you will need to make a decision on what to do with your 401(k). The options are to take the money and run, leave the 401(k) in your employers account, or roll the money over into your personal IRA account.

Unfortunately, many of you will be tempted to take the money and run. After all, everyone has many worthwhile projects and desires to entice them to spend the money. But you must resist at all cost. First of all you will have to pay tax on the money as ordinary income. Then, you will likely scuttle your retirement savings and make it almost impossible to meet your retirement goals. So the worst thing you could do is to take the cash.

Leaving the funds in your employer's 401(k) is an acceptable approach. The advantage is that it will continue to grow tax-deferred and you will be able to take the money out if you retire at age 55 (not 59 ½) or later without paying a penalty. But you will need to pay taxes on 100% of the amount whenever you withdraw it. Waiting until 70 ½ to begin a phased withdrawal will allow it to continue to grow tax-deferred for many more years.

Moving the funds into your personal IRA, termed a "rollover", is probably the best approach. It's preferable to have the majority of your tax-deferred money in one place so you can easily monitor and control it. In this way, you can also simplify asset allocation and diversification. For example, you could invest the entire IRA account in an appropriate target-date fund rather than leaving the funds scattered around in different investments. Again the choice is yours.

The custodian of your IRA will lead you through the details of making the rollover. It's pretty simple. You must avoid personally taking control of the money during the rollover. For instance, if your employer cuts you a check, they will be required to withhold 20% for taxes. Thus your best move is to have your employer cut a check directly to the custodian of your IRA account. Remember, any money you personally take out, will be treated like a taxable distribution, subject to taxes and early-withdrawal penalties. There could be difficulty in transferring company stock held in your 401(k), which may be taxable upon transfer. But don't lose sleep over this since the IRA custodians are well versed in making this happen smoothly.

Myth No. 12—Nobody Should Manage His Own Retirement Account

Stocks, bonds, small cap, and large cap—what does it all mean? Those who don't understand anything about investing feel it's hopeless. They take advice from buddies at work who claims to have made a lot of money with an investment advisor who doesn't even charge for his service. Wouldn't it be foolish not to utilize this advisor?

REALITY: Fools rush in . . . . Believe it or not, you're looking for trouble. You need to get yourself educated in a hurry. Build upon what you already know.

It's likely that your first real investment decision was, or will be, making a choice through your employer defined retirement account, i.e. 401(k). No doubt the office "experts" will volunteer advice and brag about how successful they've been. Some of them might even know what they're talking about. But fear not. Most company plans are designed to minimize the choices you have, so that you can't make a colossal mess of your account. You can still make poor choices but that's still better than staying on the sidelines.

Upon starting a new job, your employer may automatically enroll you in their 401(k) and might even automatically raise your contribution level each year unless you opt out. You might choose to direct your money into diversified investments, such as life-cycle or target-date funds. These are ideal for the novice investor or someone who never made an investment decision in their life. You will wind up with a decent portfolio and probably beat out the performance of the office experts if you take this approach

A worker's first financial advice is often via co-workers or relatives who know brokers or insurance agents, or other "experts" whose cards read "Financial Advisor." Their advice may even be free. But don't take advantage of this kind of service. They make their living by selling high-commission products such as variable annuities, cash-value life insurance, and high-fee mutual funds. They may believe that they're representing you, but their investment products will make them rich and not you. So beware of investment advisors who may not represent your interests, solely.

There's a lot of trustworthy professional help out there if you want it. Typically the mutual fund custodian of your employer's plan will provide some guidance, explaining the relative risks associated with different choices in the plan. Once you have a fair sum of money in your 401(k) combined with your IRA or other personal accounts it will probably pay you to seek out a true Certified Financial Planner.

Myth No. 13—Buy and Hold is for Suckers

Investors who are always buying into the "hot" sectors seem to make all the money. Since things are always changing, it is not a good idea to leave money sit in one investment for a long period.

REALITY: Think again. Nobody has a crystal ball.

How should you react when you're faced with a bear (down) market? Like many investors you will believe the stories of impending doom and take definitive action. However, in most cases, doing nothing is usually best. As long as your reasons for investing in the first place haven't changed and you have prepared for the possibility of down markets by holding a balanced portfolio of stocks, bonds, and cash investments, you should just stand pat.

Experienced investors understand that investing is not about jumping in and out of the market based on short-term movements. Savvy investors just stick to their asset allocation plan. They may rebalance their portfolios to maintain their target balance of stocks, bonds, and cash investments, but they don't abandon their plan.

One of the most common mistakes investors make during a bear market is to get scared or lose patience and sell as prices continue to drop. This usually assures you will be selling low. Another mistake, often made in the early stages of a bear market, is to "buy on the dip" by moving bonds or cash investments into stocks in anticipation of a quick rebound. It is almost impossible to differentiate a dip from the start of a bear market. Read the "expert" opinions and you will find they don't agree with each other. So what chance do you have to make the right move?

A bull (up) market presents the exact opposite temptations. The buy-and-hold philosophy is equally difficult to follow in bull markets, when the temptation is to move money into the "winning" sectors. Unfortunately, yesterday's winners are not likely to be tomorrow's winners. The net effect is that you will be buying at a high price. Hence, chasing these hot sectors tends to result in poor performance. The buy and hold philosophy may not be appropriate for the more aggressive investors but it'll keep the novice investor from always looking in the rear view mirror and buying high and selling low.

Myth No. 14—Constantly Tinker with Your Investments to Maximize Returns

You can improve your return by closely watching your investments and tweaking the portfolio as things change, which can be quite often. Since the financial world always seems to be in a state of flux, you need to stay close to a computer to avoid major losses and maximize returns.

REALITY: No and No. In fact, tinker too much and you could end up doing more harm than good! Your retirement funds should always be extensively allocated and diversified. You'll have no reason to make frequent changes if this is the case. When you've got your plan in gear, you should be able to sit back and just relax.

If you manage your own investments, all you really need to do is minor maintenance on a quarterly basis. Pick any day for your review. How about the last day of the quarter? This will be the time to correct for the fact that during the year, gains in some areas and losses in others threw your asset mix out of balance. Compare your current allocations with your targets. If they are off by, say 5% or more, transfer enough money out of your winners into your losers to get back to your original mix. This approach results in your selling high and buying low—the very definition of smart investing. In most plans, you can rebalance your account with one phone call to your 401(k) provider or just do it yourself online. If you invest through target-date-funds the rebalancing will be done for you automatically. Just set it and forget it.

You may have taken on too much risk if you find that market downturns give you sleepless nights. Consider shifting to a more conservative asset mix by moving much of your money from stock funds to bond funds and then leave them alone until next year. In addition, perform an annual reevaluation of whether your plan is getting you to where you need to be. If you are not reaching your goal, do not immediately decide to take more risk. Consider how much money you've added to your investments over the past year and decide what spending corrections you will make to increase the funds you are saving.

Myth No. 15—Buy Only the Proven Stock Market Winners

The stock pickers select a few of the best stocks and make high returns. Those with limited resources shouldn't sit with the same old stocks and make chicken feed. They should use their money to buy these "winners".

REALITY: Trying to pick tomorrows winners is tougher than you think. The high returns that advisors brag about are based on purchasing and then selling at the appropriate time. However, if you purchase stocks that have already had a good run up, you could very well be buying at the high which is never a good way to make money.

When you sell your losers and use the money to chase the highest-returning investments, you often end up buying at the top and selling your losers at their bottom. This phenomenon known as "looking in the rear view mirror" is a poor way to invest and has been demonstrated to significantly reduce your return over the long run. That's why you want to pick an asset mix (or target date fund) that you can stick with through market gyrations.

You don't need to have the stock-picking skills of Warren Buffett to build your nest egg. You just need to properly allocate and diversify your assets. You can use a professional advisor to tailor your holdings, rely on target-date-funds, or make up your own mix of funds. Selecting individual stocks is probably not a good idea for the novice investor, until he has been following the stock market for a number of years. If you manage your own money, stick with low-cost no-load mutual funds which let you keep more of the returns and consider using index funds which mimic specific market sectors. Just create a blend of assets that's aggressive enough to improve your odds of earning a significant return that beats inflation, but not so risky that you'll panic during market downturns and bail out at the wrong time. This may sound difficult in its own right, but most 401(k)s offer a simple and perfectly prudent solution utilizing target-date retirement funds. These funds, which invest in stocks, bonds, and other assets, create a portfolio geared to someone who plans to retire in a particular "target" year. Just pick the fund whose target date is closest to your desired retirement date and you'll be able to relax because everything is working on auto-pilot.

Myth No. 16—It's Easy to Pick Stocks

Those who follow the stock market for many years and know how to read a corporate financial statement feel like they can recognize a "good" company. There's no reason they can't pick out great individual stocks and make plenty of money.

REALITY: There is a big difference between recognizing a good company and making a sound investment. It is not too difficult to select a good company with a bright future. However it is hard to be sure that the company's stock is appropriately priced.

Buying the best company stock at too high a price is no way to build wealth. Keeping in mind that the stock market tends to price a stock on what the professional investors see as it's true value, it's going to be difficult for you to find a real bargain. And so the quality of the company is generally reflected in the price of the stock.

We all make mistakes. But when they involve retirement, serious mistakes can mean working 'til you drop instead of retiring in style. Invest too conservatively? You could fall short of cash in retirement. Invest too aggressively? A market downturn could wipe out your savings. Unless you are a seasoned investor, don't place too much of your investments in individual stocks that you personally manage. Find out as much as you can about investing. It pays to be educated.

It's okay to take a small percentage of your nest egg and try your hand at investing. But keep in mind that even financial professionals—people who are paid for the wisdom of their judgments—commit financial blunders they live to regret. Some of their errors lead to huge losses. Still, if you just invest a modest sum, your financial mistakes won't be fatal to your retirement, and you will learn from them.

Perhaps the most difficult aspect of stock trading is determining when to sell. The biggest mistake is waiting too long to sell. If the stock is going up, you'll be tempted to hold onto it and get the full thrust of the gains. If the stock is going down you'll be tempted to hold it in an effort to break-even or maybe even buy more to lower the break-even price. Each of these can be a big mistake. If you want a portfolio of individual stocks, your best bet is to use a well-known investment advisor who will make sure you sell according to plan.

Myth No. 17—Ride the Company Stock to Success

The President of a company just announced that the company will do even better next year. Many employees of the company have made a lot of money by investing their entire 401(k) accounts in the company's stock. Isn't this a good idea?

REALITY: Think twice because you don't realize the risk you are taking. Then avoid putting all your eggs in one basket. You may have full confidence in your company's future, but when it comes to your 401(k) strategy, nothing can trip you up more than blind loyalty.

Never put more than 10% of your money in your employer's stock. After all, your job security already depends on your firm's financial health. If you load up your 401(k) with your company stock, you are wagering your retirement security on your employer as well. Yes, if the stock soars, you'll do better than if you had spread your money around. But you can't afford to take the risk.

Enron is the most publicized example of just how much trouble your company can get you into. The company imploded after its executives allegedly engaged in various acts of malfeasance. The employees lost their jobs and also saw their retirement funds, heavily invested in Enron stock, shrink to almost nothing. The employees, who were encouraged to maintain their investments by assurances from the company president lost almost everything. But corporate shenanigans aren't the only reason a company's stock might take a major hit. A company with perfectly honest management might fall on hard times because of incompetent management, or the company may be the victim of economic forces over which the managers have no control. For example, an influx of cheaper products from abroad or just new technology could make their product line obsolete. The fact is that American corporate history is bursting with examples of companies that once were among the mighty and rode high on the economic landscape but later found themselves struggling for their very existence. Just look at Ford and General Motors today.

Limiting company stock in your investment portfolio is now a well accepted principle in the financial community. Even companies that require an employee to take the 401(k) company match in company stock now generally have provisions that employees over 50 years of age can redirect some if not all of their company stock. It is no longer acceptable for a company to require a 401(k) participant to put the employee's share of the plan in company stock.

Myth No. 18—Savings Accounts Are A Great Place to Put Money

You need a substantial sum of money in your savings or checking account in case you lose your job or have unexpected medical bills.

REALITY: Allowing a large sum to sit in your personal checking or savings account is a sure way to lose out. It is understandable to feel you need a fair amount of cash around for that "rainy day". However there are a number of ways to provide the liquidity you want without accepting 1 or 2% returns.

There are a number of investment vehicles that are almost as liquid as your own checking account. This includes money market mutual funds as well as some bond funds. They pay a much higher interest rate than your checking account and still allow you access to your cash in just a day or two. Some of these accounts even allow check-writing privileges. However, you can't totally replace your personal low interest rate checking account, since you are limited on the number of checks you can write in a given period. But you could certainly use it to withdraw living expenses or pay a large credit card or hospital bill every so often.

A good strategy is to maintain a small checking account to cover those monthly bills that you "love" so much. There is no reason to have a savings account. Have your paycheck deposited directly into your checking account to cover regular bills and allow for the account balance to grow, since your goal needs to be to spend less than you earn. Then periodically write a check to your IRA or personal investment account for the excess. In this way, you are not only paying the electric and gas companies but also paying yourself.

Myth No. 19—Your House Can Finance Your Retirement

Why not delay saving for retirement since you have plenty of equity in your home and can always sell it and live off the proceeds? It's easy to turn home equity into cash by selling the house and downsizing to a condo or renting an apartment, house or condo. It sure seems like a simple solution

REALITY: No, it's not that simple. With your home probably the best investment you have, considering it a retirement account is an easy trap to fall into. With the housing market in recent doldrums, the five-year real estate bull market has likely left most people house-rich. Today many people approaching retirement have a good percentage of their wealth tied up in their principal residence and are tempted to consider it as their main retirement asset. But will the strategy work? Yes, but probably not that well. Remember you still have to live somewhere. Many retirees prefer to just stay put if possible.

There are a variety of ways to get cash out of your house without moving out. These include home equity loans, mortgage refinancing, and reverse mortgages. Home equity loans are normally paid back over an agreed upon time frame. Refinancing is only appropriate if the new mortgage rate is significantly lower than the one you have now. Homeowners, at or near retirement age, who have paid off their mortgages or have only small mortgage balances remaining, are eligible to participate in most reverse mortgage programs.

Equity loans allow homeowners to borrow against the equity in their homes but usually get less than the full value. For homeowners ages 62 to 69, lenders will typically let you borrow around 60% of your home equity. You can receive payments in a lump sum, on a monthly basis, or on as a line of credit. Refinancing, at a significantly lower rate, can allow you to withdraw some cash from your home while maintaining roughly the same monthly payments.

With reverse mortgages, the bank pays you monthly. You are not obligated to pay back the money since the house is used as collateral. When you pass away or move out, the loan is paid off by the sale of the house. This may mean that you will not be able to pass the home on to your children. But homeowners whose circumstances change can restructure their payment options. Reverse mortgages tend to have significant costs and fees that tend to make this an undesirable alternative.

The best way to look at your house is as if you are never going to leave, as a place to live not a retirement account. But at the same time it makes a great insurance policy.

Myth No. 20—Spouses Just Don't Understand These Things

A spouse is always busy working and taking care of the kids. She doesn't want to be bothered with financial problems. She depends on her husband to do the right thing.

REALITY: Developing and executing a plan is something that will require cooperation between partners. Both need to be on the same page all the time.

During your working years, you will be trying to save by cutting expenses. Later on in retirement, when you are on a fixed income, you need to live within your means. Remember, that with limited retirement income, there is no opportunity to make up for spilt milk in the retirement years. You can't succeed in either of these stages if your spouse is not in there fighting alongside you instead of fighting with you. You must openly discuss all issues with your spouse so that there is mutual buy-in every step of the way. Since budgeting is probably a new experience for both parties, it could put quite a strain on a marriage. Communicating these issues effectively will be quite a challenge but absolutely essential.

What sense does it make to have one person making her own clothes for both herself and the children if the other person is visiting the casino and going drinking with the boys three nights a week? Should one partner get up an hour earlier to take public transportation to work if their spouse is having her hair done at the beauty parlor every week? Be fair. There is a natural tendency to place blame with the other party. You are both equally responsible for staying in control of your spending. Mastering this will have the added benefit in that working together to control costs will actually bring you closer together.

Myth No. 21—Nobody Can Control Death Or Taxes

Taxes are outside of your control. So just have your taxes done annually and pay what you owe the governmment and stop whining. After all there's nothing you can do about it, anyway.

REALITY:. Believe it or not, there is much you can do to affect your taxes. Adjusting your investments to minimize taxes can impact how you grow your nest egg. As you approach and enter retirement you will need to adjust your investments to minimize your taxes.

Controlling your investments with an eye on taxes is a perplexing issue for most people. Starting out you will probably have almost all your investments in tax-deferred accounts via a 401(k) through your employer and your own personal IRA. Once you've taken maximum advantage of tax-deferred accounts you will be creating your own personal investment accounts. This is the point that you need to become aware of the tax situation.

During the working years, it is appropriate to keep the majority of tax-deferred money in investments with potentially high returns since they would grow tax-free. This also permits the investor to sell shares without a tax impact at the time of the trade. The more conservative dividend paying investments should normally be kept in taxable accounts.

Retirement is a good time to review how your investments are allocated among your taxable and tax-deferred accounts. You may be surprised to find that the investment tax strategies that worked well while you were saving for retirement could work against you when you start withdrawing your money. Once retired, conventional wisdom dictates that you should first withdraw money from your taxable accounts to fund your retirement. That allows your IRAs and other tax-deferred accounts to continue to compound tax-free for as long as possible. However this is not as simple as it seems. All money ultimately withdrawn from tax-deferred accounts will be taxed as ordinary income (possibly as much as 35% depending on your retirement tax bracket). Withdrawing from a non-deferred account could allow you to claim a long term capital gain which would have a much lower tax rate (presently 15%).

Sometimes it pays to withdraw funds earlier to prevent a larger tax bill later depending on what bracket you expect to be in later on. You must keep in mind that the government could increase the capital gains tax in the future resulting in a bigger tax hit when you finally sell non-deferred investments subject to long term capital gains.

If you tap your retirement funds before age 59 1/2, you'll owe a 10% early-withdrawal penalty on top of the federal and state income taxes you'll pay on each distribution. There are exceptions that let you withdraw your money early without a penalty—but only if you follow certain rules. For example, if you are at least 55 when you leave your job, you can take distributions from your 401(k) without paying a penalty (but you will still owe income taxes on your withdrawals). You may want to keep your money in your employer's plan when you leave, if you're under the age of 55, since you'll lose the "55-and-out" option if you transfer it to your IRA.

The rules get very complicated. It's no wonder that almost everybody needs to have a tax accountant.

Myth No. 22—Everybody Needs A Lot of Life Insurance

Those who have difficulty saving money, think it's necessary to purchase cash value life insurance along with long-term care insurance. They may speak to a number of insurance agents who will all agree that these are essential.

REALITY: Listening to insurance agents is a good way to stay poor all your life. Certain types of insurance are necessary during the early years of a growing family. But they become less essential as the children age. Also there are a number of alternative ways to provide suitable protection for less cost.

Life insurance salespeople will tell you that you need cash value life insurance as a means of saving money as well as protecting your family. Although your family needs the protection, this is a very inefficient way to save. It is expected that after reading this book, you are able to control your expenses and invest appropriately to build your own cash value. You should be able to grow your assets by much more than an insurance company, with their very concervative investments. Your insurance returns might just barely compensate for inflation if you're lucky. Term insurance, with no cash value is considerably less costly, while providing the same protection. Having the savings in insurance premiums to invest will likely turn out to be far more beneficial in the long run.

A retiree with no dependents, except a spouse, generally does not need to purchase life insurance. However, if you already have a cash value policy, it may pay to keep up the premiums rather than canceling the policy. You will need to evaluate the pros and cons of continuing the policy.

There are companies that offer to buy your life insurance policies from you. They offer you cash in exchange for making them the beneficiaries. They are looking to take advantage of a retuirees need for cash. Don't do this without checking with your policy's beneficiary first.

Health insurance is essential. Everybody, except maybe the very rich, needs health insurance. If you can't get coverage through your employer, look into policies with large upfront deductibles to keep the premiums down and still protect you against the costs associated with a major health setback. Those uninsured often find themselves doomed to poor medical care if anything goes really wrong.

Auto and home insurance is also essential. Auto insurance is a State requirement and insurance on your home will be required if you still have an outstanding balance on your mortgage. You also need the protection these policies provide against being sued for all your assets should someone get hurt badly in an auto accident or should they fall on your property.

Retrospective

The anecdotes and examples described above cover a broad range of popular misconceptions. None of these are ridiculous, but quite normal. Your review of these myths should give you a good overview of the information we have covered in this book. If you didn't understand many of the principles described in this chapter, you should not hesitate to go back and once again read the passages that covered these subjects.

If this chapter made good sense to you, it is clear that you understand the approach and are ready to be successful. So it is now time to move your retirement train onto the right track and **GO FOR IT!!!!!!**

Property of
Congregation Beth Shalom
Library
772 West 5th Ave.
Naperville, IL 60543-2948